SAILING SHIP RIGS AND RIGGING

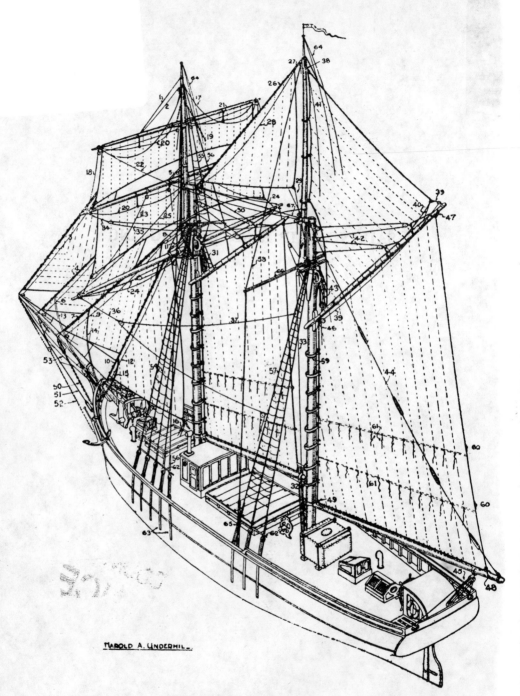

HAROLD A. UNDERHILL.

TWO-MAST TOPSAIL SCHOONER.

Perspective Drawing showing Masts, Spars, Sails and Gear.

For key to numbers see page 106.

For names of sails see page 94

Frontispiece

SAILING SHIP RIGS

AND

RIGGING

WITH AUTHENTIC PLANS OF FAMOUS VESSELS OF THE NINETEENTH AND TWENTIETH CENTURIES

BY

HAROLD A. UNDERHILL

M.C., A.M.I.E.S.

WITH ILLUSTRATIONS AND PLANS BY THE AUTHOR

GLASGOW
BROWN, SON & FERGUSON, LTD., Nautical Publishers
4-10 DARNLEY STREET

First Edition	–	1938
Second Edition	–	1955
Reprinted	–	1963
Reprinted	–	1969
Reprinted	–	1974
Reprinted	–	1978
Reprinted	–	1988

20164 7 104566 12

ISBN 0 85174 176 2

© 1988 BROWN, SON & FERGUSON, LTD., GLASGOW G41 2SD
Made and Printed in Great Britain

PREFACE

MY aim in producing this book is twofold: to enable those not already familiar with the subject to understand and identify the different rigs; and to place on record an example of each rig in the form of an authentic sail plan. This latter section will, I hope, be of interest to all lovers of the sailing ship, and prove a welcome addition to their collections of authentic data.

In compiling the sail plans from the original builders' drawings and specifications, and in some cases personal survey of the actual vessels, I have included the lead of the running gear—a feature not usually found in such drawings, but one which, I think, adds much interest and helps to bring out the individuality of the vessel. Some of the plans have been loaned for this book by designers and owners, and I am deeply indebted to them for their assistance in this matter; acknowledgment of such loans have been made on the reproductions.

It is intended to limit this volume to the classification of rigs and their variations, and no mention will be made of the numerous types of craft to be found under each rig. For this reason no deck plans, lines, or hull details have been given; further, as stated on the title page, this work only includes rigs of the later period.

I am including a number of diagrams explaining the naming of the masts, spars, sails and rigging of modern vessels, together with drawings which I hope will help towards an understanding of the use of some of the running gear. This last section is merely an elementary introduction to the subject, an outline of the basic principles which have been covered in detail in *Masting & Rigging*, a book providing full constructional drawings and descriptions of all masts and spars for both wood and steel built ships, and which follows both standing and running rigging from masthead to deck and from sail to belaying pin, including a full description of all blocks, fairleads and pins used. A full belaying-pin layout is also included.

HAROLD A. UNDERHILL.

December, 1937.
Glasgow.

CONTENTS

SECTION I.

SECTION II.

SECTION III.

SECTION IV.

Blank Sheets for Reader's own Notes and Records at End of Book

LIST OF ILLUSTRATIONS

LIST OF DRAWINGS AND DIAGRAMS.

SECTION I.
A Description of the Various Rigs.

FOUR-MAST SHIP.

THREE-MAST SHIP.

Ship.—A ship is a vessel having three or more masts and fully square-rigged throughout. Each mast is composed of a lower-mast, topmast, topgallant-mast, and in most cases royal-mast. In all ships of the later period the top-gallant and royal masts were in one single spar; see diagram on page 86. Many of the clipper ships also carried skysail-masts above the royals. The illustrations above show vessels with double topgallants and royals. The largest **ship-rigged** vessel ever built was the five-master *Preussen*.

See Sail Plans on pages 18 to 27.

FIVE-MAST BARQUE.

THREE-MAST BARQUE.

Barque.—A barque is a vessel of three or more masts; fore-and-aft rigged on the aftermost one and fully square-rigged on the remainder. In construction and number of sails carried, the square-rigged masts are the same as those of a ship. The upper illustration shows the five-mast auxiliary barque *France*, an example of the stump-topgallant rig; while the lower one is a typical three-mast barque with single topgallants and royals.

See Sail Plans on pages 28 to 37.

3

SIX-MAST BARQUENTINE.

THREE-MAST BARQUENTINE.

Barquentine.—A barquentine is a vessel having three or more masts, fully square-rigged on the fore-mast and fore-and-aft rigged on the remainder. The top illustration shows a six-mast barquentine with double topsails, double topgallants and royal; the lower sketch is of a small wooden three-mast barquentine with double topsails, single topgallant and royal.

See Sail Plans on pages 38 and 40.

FOUR-MAST JACKASS BARQUE.

THREE-MAST JACKASS BARQUE.

Jackass-Barque or **Jackass-Rig.**—These terms may be said to cover any unusual combination of masts or sails. The upper illustration shows a vessel with two square-rigged and two fore-and-aft rigged masts. One well-known craft so rigged was the old *Olympic*, built at Bath, Maine, in 1892. This rig is also called a brig-schooner. The lower sketch is of another well-known type and is claimed to have been a very handy rig; it brings to mind at once the little 500-ton tea-clipper *Ziba*, built by Hall of Aberdeen in 1858, and the more recent *Sabrina*, of 1876. Many other titles have been used to describe these rigs, such as "Hermaphrodite-barques, Jigger-barques," etc., perhaps because those who were fond of the ships objected to the name jackass being applied to their favourites.

5

BRIG.

Brig.—A brig is a two-masted vessel, fully square-rigged on both masts. In construction and number of sails carried, the masts are the same as those of a full-rigged ship. In a brig the spanker or main-trysail (see page 93) is set on the lower main-mast.

See Sail Plan on page 42.

SNOW.

Snow.—A snow is a brig as described above, but the spanker, or main-trysail, sets on a small try-sail mast or pole just abaft the main lower-mast. This try-sail mast reaches from the main-top to a step on the deck, and forms a track on which the spanker mast hoops slide.

See Sail Plan on page 44.

BRIGANTINE (Original Rig).

Brigantine.—The true brigantine is a two-masted vessel having a fully square-rigged fore-mast, and a fore-and-aft rigged main-mast with square-sails on the topmast. This rig does not seem to have been used to any great extent, and the term brigantine is now used to describe such a vessel as above but without the square sails on the main-mast.

See below.

HERMAPHRODITE BRIG (now termed a brigantine).

Hermaphrodite Brig.—This rig has a fully rigged fore-mast, and fore-and-aft rigged main; it is the same as the true brigantine but without the square topsails on the main. The term hermaphrodite brig is no longer in use and this rig is now known as a brigantine.

See Sail Plans on pages 46 and 48.

FIVE-MAST TWO-TOPSAIL SCHOONER.

TWO-MAST TWO-TOPSAIL SCHOONER.

Two-topsail Schooner or Main-Topsail Schooner.—This rig originally applied to two-masted vessels, fore-and-aft rigged on both masts, and having square topsails on both topmasts as illustrated by the lower sketch. In 1921 Messrs. F. A. Vinnen launched the first of a fleet of five auxiliary steel five-mast schooners; these vessels carried square sails on the fore and mizen topmasts, as will be seen in the upper sketch which shows the *Susanne Vinnen*. All five were alike, and there seems to be some doubt as to the correct name for their rig. In my opinion they should come under the classification of two-topsail schooners, which is certainly preferable to such cumbersome efforts as "a three-mast schooner chasing a two-mast schooner."

THREE-MAST TOPSAIL SCHOONER.

TWO-MAST TOPSAIL SCHOONER.

Topsail Schooner.—The topsail schooner is a vessel of two or more masts; fore-and-aft rigged throughout, but with square-sails on the fore topmast. They differ from barquentines and brigantines in the construction and rig of the fore-mast; the schooner's fore-mast consists of a lower-mast and topmast, and sets a gaff fore-sail; while the fore-mast of a barquentine or brigantine has lower-mast, topmast, topgallant-mast and royal-mast, these latter vessels also carry staysails between the fore and main instead of the gaff fore-sail of the schooner. The upper sketch shows a three-mast topsail schooner, and the lower a two-mast topsail schooner.

See Sail Plans on pages 50 to 56.

9

SEVEN-MAST FORE-AND-AFT SCHOONER.

TWO-MAST FORE-AND-AFT SCHOONER.

Fore-and-aft Schooner.—This rig has two or more masts, all fore-and-aft rigged. The largest fore-and-aft schooner ever built was the seven-masted *Thomas W. Lawson* shown in the upper sketch.

See Sail Plans on pages 58 to 62.

10

STAYSAIL SCHOONER.

BERMUDA SCHOONER (Composite Rig).

Staysail Schooner and Bermuda Schooner.—In the staysail schooner all canvas, with the exception of the main, is set on fore-and-aft stays and saves the weight of spars aloft. It is also claimed that this type of canvas will set much better than that of the old gaff-rigged schooners. At present this rig is largely used by yachts, although the Sail Plan on page 64 shows the rig used in a trading vessel. The upper sketch shows a typical staysail-schooner yacht while the lower one indicates a composite rig which is quite common in American waters; the fore-mast is gaff-rigged and the main Bermuda.

11

KETCH.

Ketch.—A ketch is a two-masted vessel having a large fore-and-aft rigged main-mast, with a smaller mizen.   The mizen mast of a ketch is stepped on the fore side of the tiller.

See Sail Plans on pages 66, 68 and 70.

YAWL.

Yawl.—The yawl rig is much the same as the ketch, but the mizen is much smaller and stepped right at the stern of the vessel and abaft the tiller.

12

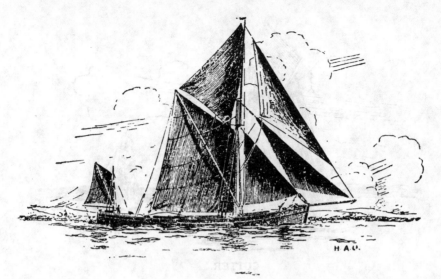

SPRIT-SAIL RIG.

Spritsail Rig.—The spritsail rig resembles the gaff-sail in shape, but is entirely different in principle.   The sail is extended by means of a spar, or sprit, running diagonally across it, and both sprit and sail remain permanently aloft· Sail is taken off by being brailed, or gathered, to the mast; these brails can be seen running across the sails in the top sketch.

The Thames barge is perhaps the best known example of the spritsail rig, and the above sketches show a barge under sail and with sails brailed up.

See Sail Plan on page 72.

13

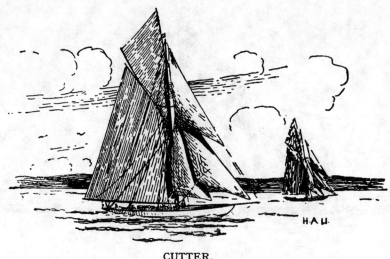

CUTTER.

Cutter.—A cutter is a vessel having one mast: she carries two or more head-sails and a gaff or Bermuda main-sail.

See Sail Plans on pages 74 to 78.

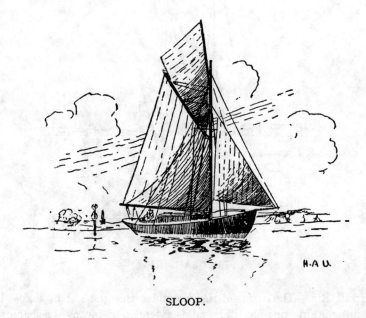

SLOOP.

Sloop.—A sloop may be said to be a cutter with a single head-sail or jib. Like the cutter, she may be Bermuda or gaff-rigged. This of course is the modern interpretation as applied to small craft. In the days of the sailing man-of-war it referred to a small class of warship, which might be any rig from a full-rigged ship to a schooner.

BERMUDA RIG.

Bermuda Rig.—The name Bermuda is given to all vessels having the modern triangular fore-and-aft sail abaft the mast, in place of the older gaff-sail. This rig is very lofty and dispenses with the weight of gaffs and topsail gear aloft.   A feature of this rig is the arrangement of spreaders and bracing necessary to support such a tall spar.   The above sketch shows, from left to right: Bermuda cutter; Bermuda yawl and Bermuda sloop.

See Sail Plans on pages 70 and 76.

CAT-BOAT.

Cat-Boat.—This rig consists of a single gaff-sail, carried on a mast, stepped right in the eyes of the boat.

FISHING LUGGER (Dipping and Standing Lugs).

SAILING CANOE (Standing Lugs).

Lug.—The lug is a fore-and-aft sail set on a yard, of which about one-third is on the fore side of the mast. The main-sail of the vessel in the upper sketch is a dipping lug; the tack of the sail is made fast to the stem head, and as the sail has to be to the leeward of the mast, it is necessary to lower the sail and hoist it again on the other side of the mast every time the boat goes about, the fore end of the yard being "dipped" round the mast in doing so. The mizen in the upper sketch, and both sails in the lower, are standing lugs; the tack of this sail is made fast to the mast and it is not necessary to dip round when going about.

16

HUMBER KEEL.

Humber Keel.—This craft is outside all the standard rigs; she carries a single mast on which are set a square main-sail and topsail. The vessels are used on the inland waterways of Yorkshire and, in spite of the rather crude looking rig, seem to be quite handy little ships.

See Sail Plan and description on pages 82 and 83.

NORFOLK WHERRY.

Norfolk Wherry.—Strictly speaking, this is not a rig but a type. The wherry is una or cat-boat rigged, but she has one very interesting feature which I think justifies mention here. Her gaff is set up with a single halliard in place of the usual peak and throat halliards. This halliard is made fast to the gaff about one quarter out from the jaws; it then passes through a double block at the masthead, out to a single block on a bridle at the peak, back through the double block and down to a single block near the jaws, back up to a sheave in the mast and so to the deck.

This arrangement can be followed in the sketch above.

SECTION II.
Sail Plans and Descriptions.

HAROLD A UNDERHILL

STEEL FIVE-MAST SHIP "PREUSSEN."

By permission of   Reederei F. Laeisz, Hamburg.

FIVE-MAST SHIP "PREUSSEN."

THE sail plan on the opposite page is of particular interest, as the *Preussen* was the only five-mast full-rigged ship ever built.

She was a steel vessel and all her masts and spars were constructed of the same material. In common with most large steel ships of the period, her lower-masts and topmasts were in one single spar, with lofty topgallant and royal-masts above. The total height of her main-mast was 223 ft. from keel to truck, while her lower and royal-yards were 102 ft. and 52·5 ft. respectively. She crossed six yards on each mast and had a sail area of about 50,000 sq. ft. in 47 sails.

An interesting feature of her mast construction was the absence of parrels on her hoisting yards. These yards were attached to shoes, which ran on iron tracks riveted to the fore side of the masts, on much the same principle as the mast track of a modern Bermuda rigged yacht.

All standing rigging was steel wire set up with rigging screws, the running gear being either flexible steel wire or hemp. I am indebted to Basil Lubbock's *Nitrate Clippers* for the following interesting details regarding the quantities of wire and gear used in her rigging:

Total length of standing rigging	35,424 ft.
„ „ wire running rigging	43,394 ft.
„ „ hemp running rigging	56,613 ft.
„ „ chain running rigging	2,296 ft.

making a total of 137,727 ft. of wire, hemp and chain aloft. To this can be added 1260 blocks and 248 rigging screws.

The *Preussen* was built in 1902 for the famous "P" Line of Herr Laeisz, and remained under his flag until her loss off Dover in 1910.

REGISTERED DETAILS.

Rig	Steel five-mast ship.
Tonnage	5081 gross.
Length	407·8 ft.
Breadth	53·6 ft.
Depth	27·1 ft.
Built	1902.
By	J. C. Tecklenborg, Geestemunde.
Owner	R. F. Laeisz ("P" Line.)
Port of Registry ..	Hamburg.
Flags	R M P T.

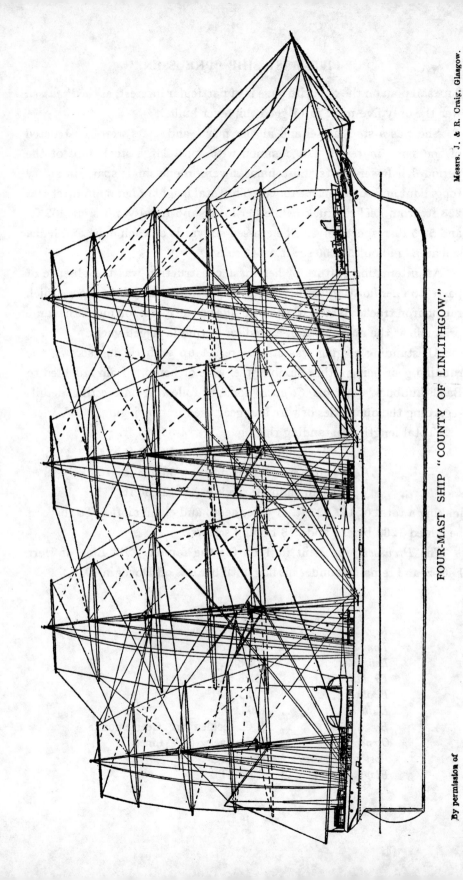

FOUR-MAST SHIP "COUNTY OF LINLITHGOW."

By permission of　　　　　　　　　　　Messrs. J. & R. Craig, Glasgow.

FOUR-MAST FULL-RIGGED SHIP "COUNTY OF LINLITHGOW."

THE four-mast full-rigged ship came into vogue about 1874, the object being to reduce the size and weight of spars aloft; they were not abnormally large, and there were many three-mast ships of equal and even greater tonnage, but the four fully square-rigged masts gave a greater distribution of sail area than would be the case with a three-mast ship of equal size. They are reputed to have been very handy vessels and easy to handle, but most of them were later converted into four-mast barques, on the grounds that this rig was more economical in gear and labour.

Between 1875 and 1887, twelve iron four-mast ships were built for Messrs. R. & J. Craig's "County" Line, or Craig's "Counties" as these ships were better known; the first being the *County of Peebles* and the last and largest the *County of Linlithgow*. The *Peebles* and her early sisters had single topsails on the jigger-mast, but the later ships, as in the case of the *Linlithgow*, were fitted with double topsails on all four masts; except for this and minor variations in dimensions, all these vessels were very much alike.

Although the spike bowsprit had been in use for many years prior to the launch of the *County of Linlithgow*, she, like all her sisters, was given a bowsprit and long jib-boom, and also carried spencers on both main and mizen.

The *County of Linlithgow* remained under Craig's flag until about 1905 when she was sold to Chilian owners. In the 1916-17 register she changes over to the American flag and her name becomes *Katherine*, with San Francisco as her home port. In 1920-21 she appears as a twin screw aux. motor ship for the same owners, and by 1929 she had passed to the Greeks.

REGISTERED DETAILS.

Rig	Iron four-mast ship.
Tonnage	2202 gross.
Length	286·9 ft.
Breadth	43·5 ft.
Depth	24·1 ft.
Built	1887.
By	Barclay, Curle & Co., Glasgow.
Owners	R. & J. Craig.
Port of Registry ..	Glasgow.

C

21

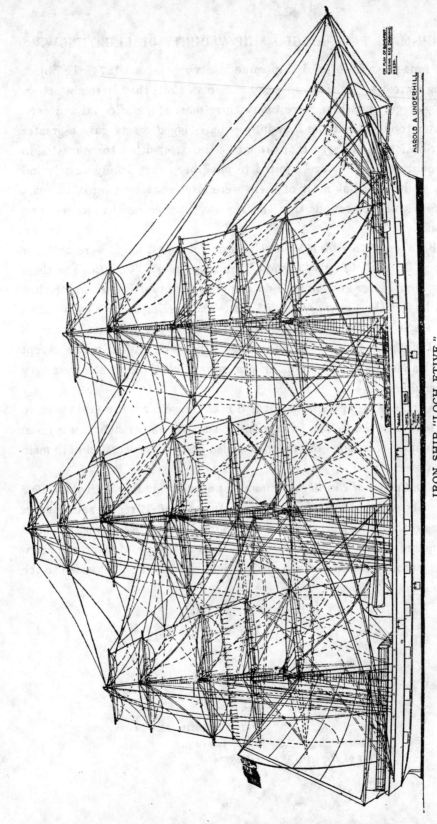

IRON SHIP "LOCH ETIVE."

HAROLD A UNDERHILL

SHIP "LOCH ETIVE."

THE *Loch Etive* and her sister ship *Loch Sunart* were fine examples of the Clyde-built clipper. Iron ships with a lofty sail plan, crossing a main skysail over single topgallants and double topsails, and staysails on all available stays, which together with the main spencer gave them a large sail plan.

The main-mast was 145 ft. from deck to truck, with a main-yard of 77·5 ft. All square sails clewed up to slings or quarters. The sail plan opposite shows the *Loch Etive's* original rig; later the jib-boom was shortened by 12 ft. and the fore-royal and fore-topgallant stays set up just outside the outer-jib stay. Towards the end of her career she was further cut down by stripping the yards off the mizen, thus converting her into a barque.

The *Loch Etive* had the distinction of carrying Joseph Conrad as third mate, and to quote his words, "She was built for hard driving and unquestionably received all the driving she could stand."

She remained under the Loch Line flag until about 1911 when she was sold to France.

REGISTERED DETAILS.

Rig	Iron ship.
Tonnage	1288 gross.
Length	226·9 ft.
Breadth	35·9 ft.
Depth	21·6 ft.
Built	1877.
By	A. & J. Inglis, Glasgow.
Owners	Loch Line. (General Shipping Co., managed by Aitken, Lilburn & Co.)
Port of Registry ..	Glasgow.
Flags	R C K B.

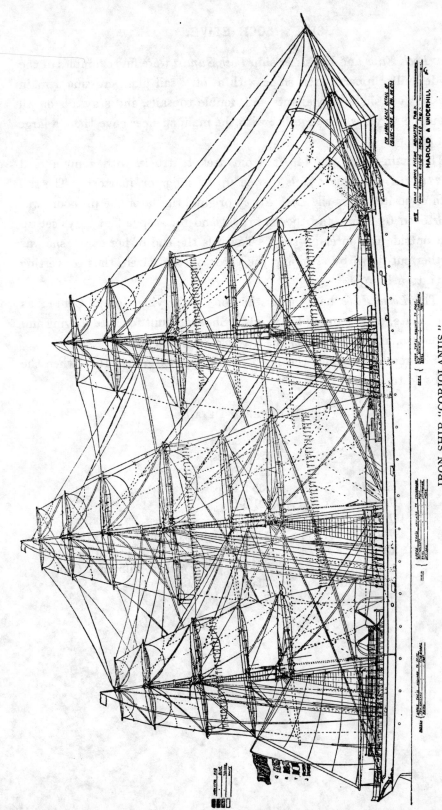

IRON SHIP "CORIOLANUS."

HAROLD A. UNDERHILL.

SHIP "CORIOLANUS."

THIS is another example of the Clyde-built clipper, and except for a little difference in cut, her sail plan is the same as that of *Loch Etive*; however, I make no excuse for including this fine vessel.

It has been said that the *Coriolanus* was one of the most beautiful iron clippers ever turned out, and it certainly is a fact that her model gained the highest award at the Shipwrights Exhibition, London, in 1877.

In hull layout she differs from the *Loch Etive*; in place of the full poop and topgallant forecastle, she has a raised quarterdeck and cabin top, or monkey poop, and her forecastle is at the level of the topgallant rail. All this gives her a clear rail fore and aft, and rather suggests a flush-decked ship.

She was later cut down to a barque, and changed her name and flag several times, but she reverted to her original name while under the American flag at the end of her career. She made her last passage during the summer of 1936, when she was towed from Bath, Maine, to Fall River, Massachusetts, to be broken up. In May, 1937, all that was left of the old ship was a foot or so of plating sticking out of the mud.

REGISTERED DETAILS.

Rig	Iron ship.
Tonnage	1053 gross.
Length	217·4 ft.
Breadth	35·2 ft.
Depth	20·1 ft.
Built	1876
By	Arch. McMillan & Son, Dumbarton.
Owner	J. Patton, Junr. & Co.
Port of Registry ..	London.
Flags . ..	Q K T J.

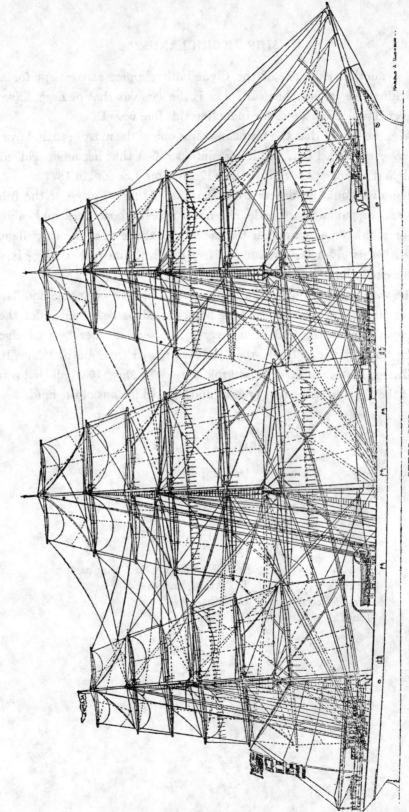

STEEL SHIP "ACAMAS."

SHIP "ACAMAS."

In the *Acamas* we have a good illustration of the big full-rigged ship, and one which makes an interesting comparison with the *Loch Etive* and *Coriolanus*. The main-skysail is absent; double instead of single topgallants are carried on each mast, and there is a marked difference in the general cut of the sail plan. The two former ships are lofty and narrow while the *Acamas* has great spread, her main and main-royal yards being 90 ft. and 40 ft. overall respectively. This spread tends to take away the lofty appearance, but as a matter of fact her main-mast is the same height as that of the *Loch Etive*, 145 ft. from deck to truck; she is of course, a larger ship.

The *Acamas* follows the modern practice of having the yards on the fore and main-masts of the same length, so that they are interchangeable in case of need. She also has the modern spike—or single spar—bowsprit in place of the bowsprit and jib-boom.

She made no claim to being a clipper, but was a steady all round carrier, and could load a deadweight cargo of 3200 tons on a draft of about 21 ft. She was taken off the stocks by Captain W. A. Nelson, and with the exception of one voyage, remained under his command during the whole of her service under the British flag.

Eventually sold to Norway, she was posted missing in 1918 on a passage from Rio to New York. Her name was then *Gezina*.

REGISTERED DETAILS.

Rig	Steel ship.
Tonnage	1860 gross.
Length	262·4 ft.
Breadth	38·9 ft.
Depth	22·9 ft.
Built	1897.
By	T. Ritson, Maryport.
Owner	T. Ritson.
Port of Registry	Maryport.
Flags	P T L J.

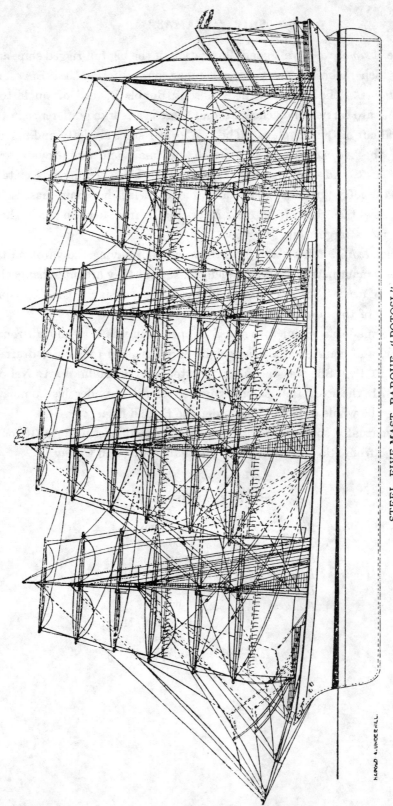

STEEL FIVE-MAST BARQUE "POTOSI."

HAROLD A. UNDERHILL.

FIVE-MAST BARQUE "POTOSI."

IN this vessel we find a strong family resemblance to the *Preussen*; she was, in fact, a product of the same yard, and built for the same owner. As will be seen from the date given below, the *Potosi* was the first of the two, being launched seven years before the *Preussen*.

On a proportionate basis the *Potosi* was the loftier vessel; her main-mast scales 212 ft. from keel to truck, with a main-yard of 96 ft. On her five masts she carried 43 working sails.

One feature of the *Potosi's* design is the division of the spanker into two sails; this was a common practice with the German builders, and will be found in most of their larger sailing vessels, although it does not seem to have been adopted by builders of any other nationality. There was one exception to this however, the Danish five-mast barque *Köben-havn*. This vessel was built at Leith in 1921 by Messrs. Ramage & Ferguson, and had a double spanker when she first came out, but later the lower gaff was discarded and a single spanker carried.

The *Potosi* was in Valparaiso in 1914 and remained there throughout the Great War. In 1918 she was handed over to the French under the terms of the Treaty of Versailles, but it was not until 1923 that she was again brought into commission, by which time she was owned in Valparaiso, and her name changed to *Flora*.

She was lost by fire in July, 1925.

REGISTERED DETAILS.

Rig	Steel five-mast barque.
Tonnage	4026 gross.
Length	366·3 ft.
Breadth	49·7 ft.
Depth	28·5 ft.
Built	1895.
By	J. C. Tecklenborg, Geestemunde.
Owners	R. F. Laeisz ("P" Line).
Port of Registry ..	Hamburg.
Flags	R K G B.

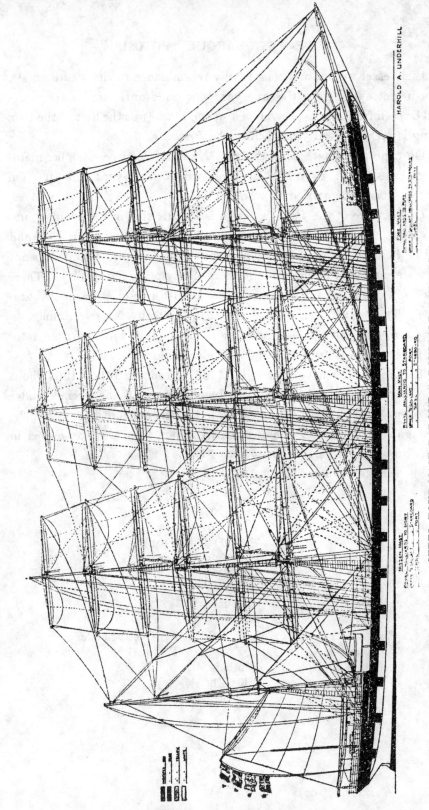

STEEL FOUR-MAST BARQUE "ARCHIBALD RUSSELL."

HAROLD A. UNDERHILL

FOUR-MAST BARQUE "ARCHIBALD RUSSELL."

THIS drawing illustrates a good example of the later day four-mast barque. The sail plan is square with great spread, and includes royals over double-topgallants and double-topsails. In common with most steel vessels of her day, the *Archibald Russell* has all her square-rigged masts of the same height and all yards interchangeable.

In my opinion, the fact of the lower-masts and topmasts being separate spars adds much to her appearance, as the absence of lower doublings always seems to give a mast a bare look.

Many of the modern steel four-mast barques have midship super-structure, as in the diagrams on pages 96 to 100, while some, such as the *Viking* and *Herzogin Cecilie*, had the poop deck extended to well forward of the main-mast, leaving only a short well deck abaft the fore-mast. However, this practice was more common with German builders, and the *Archibald Russell* may be taken as a typical example of the British four-mast barque.

She is a Clyde product, built by Scott's of Greenock, and it is interesting to note that she was one of the last large square-riggers to be built on the river.

The *Archibald Russell* remained in commission until the Second World War when under the ownership of Captain Erikson of Mariehamn, she was caught in a British port. There she remained throughout the war, dismantled and used as a store ship. By 1954 the days of the commercial sailing ship were over, and she did not go to sea again.

REGISTERED DETAILS.

Rig	Steel four-mast barque.
Tonnage	2385 gross.
Length	291·4 ft.
Breadth	43·2 ft.
Depth	24·1 ft.
Built	1905.
By	Scott's Shipbuilding & Engineering Co., Greenock.
Owner	J. Hardie & Co.
Port of Registry ..	Glasgow.
Flags	H C B F.

Note:—The drawing opposite shows her flag hoist of T P Q R under the ownership of Captain Erikson.

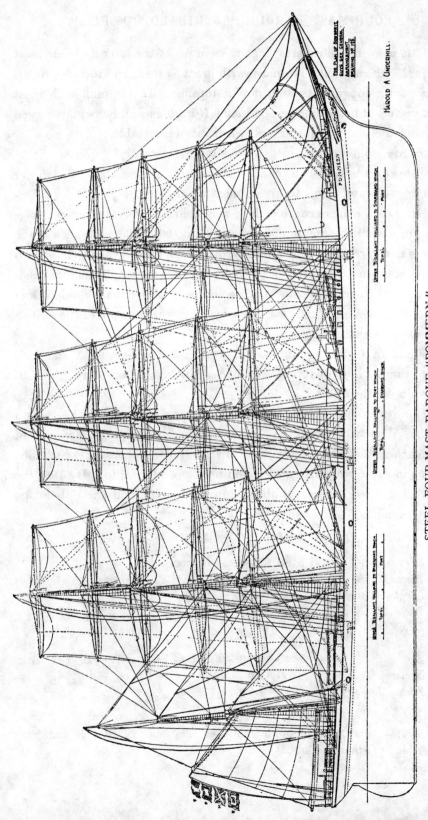

STEEL FOUR-MAST BARQUE "POMMERN."

HAROLD A UNDERHILL.

FOUR-MAST BARQUE "POMMERN."

THE sailing ship owners' first effort towards economy in running cost was the introduction of double-topsails and later double-topgallants; which, by dividing the sails into smaller units, enabled the vessels to be worked by smaller crews. However, as steam competition increased, further saving became necessary. This led to the elimination of royals and all lighter sails and so the bald-header, or stump-topgallant rig, came into being.

Many existing ships were cut down by stripping off the royals and skysails, while certain new craft were launched as bald-headers; the *Pommern* is an example of the latter.

Her lower-masts and topmasts are in one piece, and every effort has been made to save labour and running expenses. All square-rigged masts are of the same height, and all yards and sails interchangeable; a great advantage when replacements or repairs were necessary. The rigging is of steel wire set up with rigging screws. Halliard winches are used for all hoisting yards and all the lower yards are controlled by brace winches.

She was launched as the *Mneme* and became the *Pommern* when taken over by Herr Laeisz for his "P" line of sailing ships.

REGISTERED DETAILS.

Rig	.. ..	Steel four-mast barque.
Tonnage	.. ..	2423 gross.
Length	.. ..	302·0 ft.
Breadth	.. ..	43·2 ft.
Depth	.. ..	24·7 ft.
Built	.. ..	1903.
By	.. ..	J. Reid & Co., Glasgow.
Owner	.. ..	F. Laeisz.
Port of Registry	..	Hamburg.
Flags	.. ..	R N C K.

Note:—The drawing opposite shows her flag hoist of T P M W as when under the ownership of Captain Erikson.

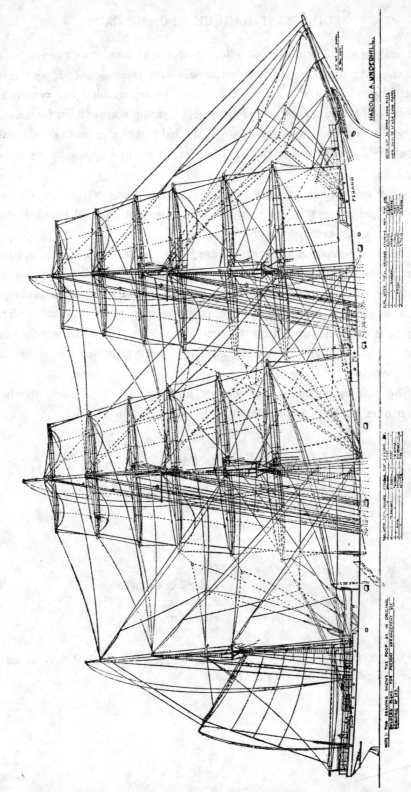

STEEL BARQUE "PENANG."

HAROLD A. UNDERHILL

NOTE: THIS DRAWING SHOWS THE POOP AS IN ORIGINAL
SHELTER PLANS FOR FREIGHT ARRANGEMENT.
DRAWING Nº 113.

THREE-MAST BARQUE "PENANG."

THE *Penang* is a modern steel three-mast barque with double-topsails and double-topgallants. She was built as the *Albert Rickmers*, and it is widely accepted that she was originally a full-rigged ship, being cut down to a barque at a later date.

I have a print off the builder's original sail and rigging plan, which leaves no room for doubt that she was designed as a barque, and I see no reason to believe that she was built otherwise. Further, examination of the actual vessel—or for that matter any photograph of her—will show that her mizen is just as designed, and certainly was never the mizen of a full-rigged ship.

I think it possible that the idea has originated from a mistake in the original entry in the register, and as she has been registered as a ship ever since, it has given rise to the opinion that she is an ex-ship cut down. This hypothesis is supported by the fact that she is still on the register as a ship, while other vessels which have been cut down from ships to barques are shown under the latter rig.

The *Penang* has a large water ballast tank mid-ships, which when pumped out can be used for stowage of cargo.

The layout on the opposite page shows the poop as originally designed; she later carried a chartroom, which was removed from the *Hougomont* when the latter was sunk as a breakwater in Australia in 1933.

REGISTERED DETAILS.

Rig	Steel three-mast barque. (Registered as ship.)
Tonnage	2039 gross.
Length	265·6 ft.
Breadth	40·1 ft.
Depth	24·7 ft.
Built	1905.
By	Rickmers. At Bremerhaven.
Owners	Rickmers Reismühlen, Rhed. & Schffb. Act. Ges.
Port of Registry .	Bremerhaven.
Flags	Q J B D.

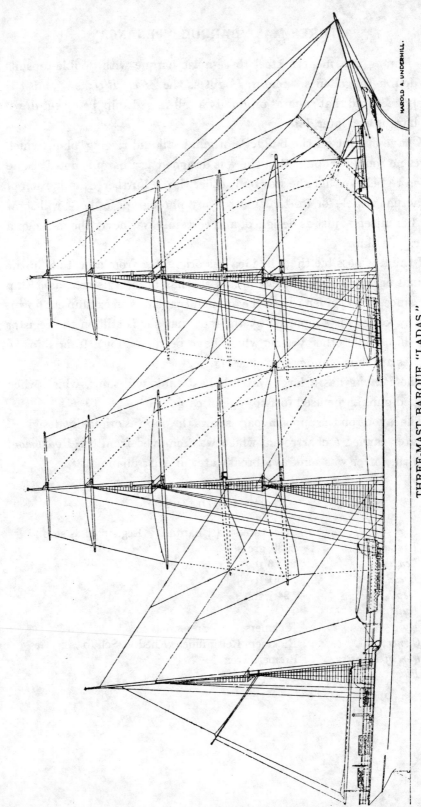

THREE-MAST BARQUE "LADAS."

HAROLD A. UNDERHILL.

THREE-MAST BARQUE "LADAS."

THE *Ladas* has a very moderate sail plan with few outstanding features but I have included it as an example of the three-mast barque with single-topgallants over double-topsails.

The drawing, which was taken from the builders' original, shows three head-sails, but the actual ship carried four, an outer-jibstay being taken from the cross-trees to the outer band on the bowsprit. The *Acamas*, which was a product of the same yard, was also designed with three head-sails but was actually sent to sea with four. The drawing on page 26 shows the latter arrangement; in fact, both the outer-jib and the main-royal staysail are additional to the original design.

It will be noticed that the square-rigged masts of the *Ladas* are built up in three spars with the usual doublings, while her mizen is a single spar from keel to truck.

Captain A. Hodgson, writing of his experiences in the *Ladas*, says that she was a most weatherly craft; a quality which saved her from destruction on her maiden voyage. Ice had been reported on either bow, and later right ahead, and it was discovered that she had sailed right into a deep bay of ice. Only her ability to claw to windward enabled her to beat clear of the bay, which she did with little to spare.

REGISTERED DETAILS.

Rig	Steel three-mast barque.
Tonnage	1395 gross.
Length	233·3 ft.
Breadth	36·9 ft.
Depth	22·0 ft.
Built	1894.
By	Ritson & Co., Maryport.
Owner ..	Ritson & Co.
Port of Registry ..	Maryport.
Flags	

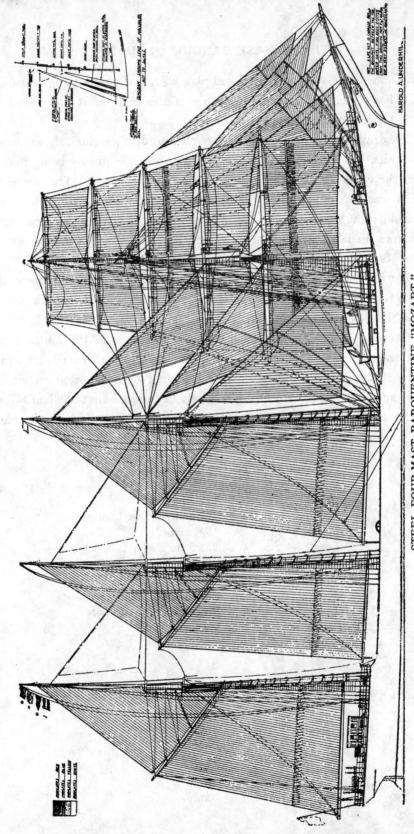

STEEL FOUR-MAST BARQUENTINE "MOZART."

HAROLD A. UNDERHILL.

FOUR-MAST BARQUENTINE "MOZART."

TOWARDS the end of the sailing ship era, designers were investigating all possible methods of reducing running costs, and one line of experiment was the development of the big steel barquentine. Fore-and-aft canvas requires less men to handle it than would be the case of a full-rigger of equal size, and it was hoped that the large barquentine would offer a solution to the problem.

A number of these vessels were turned out, and the *Mozart* will serve as a good illustration of the type. She was a large craft and heavily sparred; her fore-mast was stump-topgallant rigged, with great spread, the lower yard being 93 ft. and the royal 53·5 ft.; the latter would have made a good main-yard for some of the earlier ships! The fore-and-aft masts were huge steel spars, all of the same height, namely 178 ft. from keel to truck.

She was well provided with winches, both steam and hand, one of the latter being a standard brace winch to operate her lower yards. The *Mozart* was one of the comparatively few sailing vessels to carry water ballast tanks as part of the hold. The ballast tank occupied most of the space between the main and mizen masts for the full width of the ship, and came up to the level of the 'tween deck. When pumped out this tank could be used for cargo stowage.

Like her sister ship *Beethoven*—which by the way was 7 feet longer, but identical in other respects—the spacing of the fore-and-aft rigged masts was unequal, which, together with the stump-topgallant rig forward, rendered her less pleasing in appearance than some of the other barquentines such as *Oberon*, *Titania*, or that beautiful creation *Tacora*. Nevertheless she was a fine vessel, and it was with great regret that I watched her rapid reduction to scrap iron when she was broken up on the Clyde in 1935.

REGISTERED DETAILS.

Rig	.. ..	Steel four-mast barquentine.
Tonnage	.. ..	2003 gross.
Length	.. ..	262·9 ft.
Breadth	.. ..	40·1 ft.
Depth	.. ..	24·2 ft.
Built	.. ..	1904.
By ..	.. ..	Grangemouth & Greenock Dockyard Co., Greenock.
Owners	..	A. C. De Freitas & Co.
Port of Registry	..	Hamburg.
Flags	.. ..	R N D J.

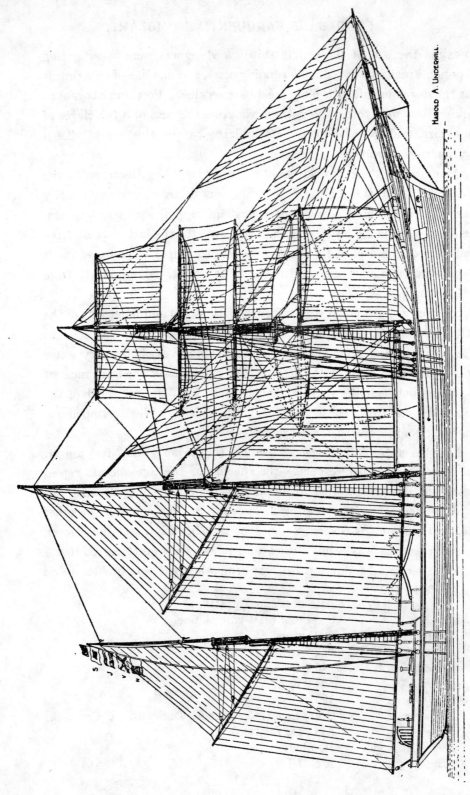

WOOD THREE-MAST BARQUENTINE "WATERWITCH."

HAROLD A. UNDERHILL.

WOOD THREE-MAST BARQUENTINE "WATERWITCH."

ALTHOUGH now barquentine-rigged the *Waterwitch* was originally a brig, and her raised quarterdeck, with its teak rail—on turned wood stanchions—at the break, and the short ladders on either side, renders it an easy matter to visualise her as such. Further traces of the old rig can be found in the sheaves for main tacks and sheets—for these are still in her bulwarks—and the arrangement of the timbers.

To-day her stern seems rather heavy and square, but it was not always so, for the square transom was only fitted when she was rebuilt. remember the late Captain Deacon telling me that at one time she had a round stern, with long overhanging counter. The drawing opposite shows the transom stern as she was when I made a survey of her in 1932.

The *Waterwitch* has a good reputation as a passage maker, with many fine runs to her credit. In her early days she had a great deal of deep-sea work in both the fruit and stock fish trades, but it is as a coaster in the Cornish china clay trade that she is best known.

In the early stages of the World War I she sank in Newlyn harbour, and remained under water until 1918, when she was raised and rebuilt.

She was in regular service until about 1936 when she was put on the mud at Par, Cornwall, where she remained for some three years and it seemed that her sailing days were over. However in 1939 she was bought by Estonian owners and in May of that year she once more set sail, this time for her new home port of Tallinn, which she reached after a passage of 44 days, and from which she once more resumed her trading.

An interesting point regarding her last few years as a British ship was the crew she carried. As a rule her forecastle complement was made up of men holding masters' certificates, who were putting in the necessary sea service in square-rig to qualify for the Trinity House Pilot Service, and as she was the only square-rigged vessel on the British coast she was never short of a crew.

REGISTERED DETAILS.

Rig	.. ..	Wood three-mast barquentine.
Tonnage	.. ..	207 gross.
Length	.. ..	112·0 ft.
Breadth	.. ..	25·8 ft.
Depth	.. ..	12·8 ft.
Built	.. ..	1871.
By ..	.. ..	Meadus, Poole.
Owners	.. ..	E. Stephens.
Port of Registry	..	Fowey.
Flags	.. ..	S J V H.

WOOD BRIG "MARIE SOPHIE."

HAROLD A UNDERHILL

WOOD BRIG "MARIE SOPHIE."

LLOYD's Register for 1853-54 is in front of me as I write, and taking several pages at random, I find that there is an average of eight or nine brigs and snows to each page of twenty-five vessels. This will give some idea of the popularity of the brig in the middle of the 19th century. The rig was to be found in both deep-sea and coasting trades, and several of the sailing coasters with us in later years started life as brigs.

The brig was also largely used in the Navy, and some of them were retained as training vessels for a long time after the coming of steam; in fact, the last of them did not go out of service until a few years before the First World War. The naval vessels were 10-gun and 16-gun brigs, of 400 to 500 tons. Many of them were over sparred, with the result that they were very tender and carned the name of "sea coffins." Naval brigs retained the single topsails right to the end, but having large crews they could handle the canvas with ease.

The *Marie Sophie* is a good example of the trading brig in her prime she has a lofty sail plan with double-topsails, and single topgallants and royals above. Built at Elsfleth in 1879 under the name of *Marie*, she changed her flag several times and came under British ownership in 1897; by this time her name had changed to *Marie Sophie*, and with Falmouth as her port of registry she continued nder uthe Red Ensign until she was lost in 1902.

REGISTERED DETAILS.

Rig	Wood brig.
Tonnage	234 gross.
Length ..	126·7 ft.
Breadth	26·2 ft.
Depth	12·8 ft.
Built	1879.
By	J. Wempe, Elsfleth.
Owners	R. J. Hockin. (After 1897.)
Port of Registry ..	Falmouth.

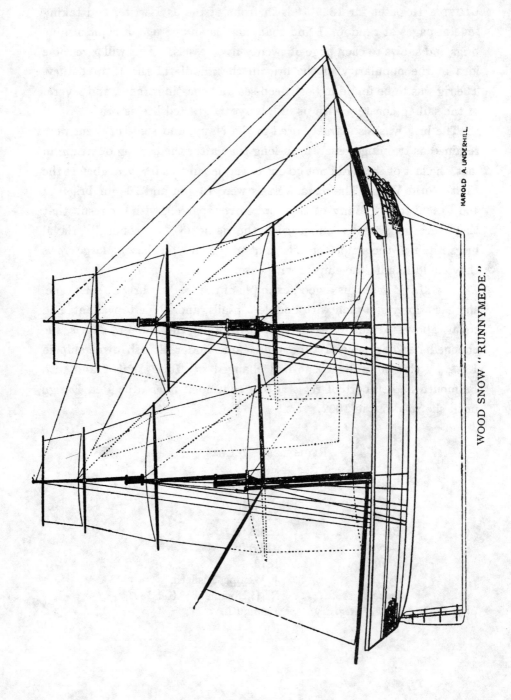

WOOD SNOW "RUNNYMEDE."

HAROLD A. UNDERHILL.

WOOD SNOW "RUNNYMEDE."

THIS drawing clearly shows the difference between the snow and the true brig. Just abaft the main lower-mast is the trysail-mast, on which the trysail—or spanker—boom and gaff jaws work, and to which the sail is laced.

The trysail-mast only extends from the deck to the main top, and is just far enough abaft the main to allow the lacing or hoops to slide freely.

There seems to be a great deal of confusion regarding this rig, due perhaps to the fact that, after about 1830, both rigs were commonly known as brigs; in fact, some of the naval brigs carried a trysail-mast and were actually snow rigged. Later it became the practice to use the term snow in connection with any snow or brig rigged vessel hailing from the Baltic.

The sail plan shows a vessel with single topsails and topgallants. This of course does not affect the classification of rig, as prior to the introduction of double-topsails in 1853 all square-rigged vessels were so rigged. Double-topgallants did not come in until about 1870.

Incidentally, it is interesting to note that wooden sailing ships, *rigged with single topsails and topgallants*, are still being built and sailed in the rice trade across the Bay of Bengal. These vessels, brigs, barquentines and barques, are built almost entirely of Malabar teak, and are native owned and manned.

In the 1853 register I find that the *Runnymede* is classified as a wood brig, the details being as under.

REGISTERED DETAILS.

Rig	.. ..	Wood brig.
Tonnage	.. ..	236 gross.
Built	.. ..	1845.
By ..	.. ..	R. Steel.
At ..	.. ..	Greenock.
Owners	.. ..	Kerrs & Co.
Port of Registry	..	Greenock.

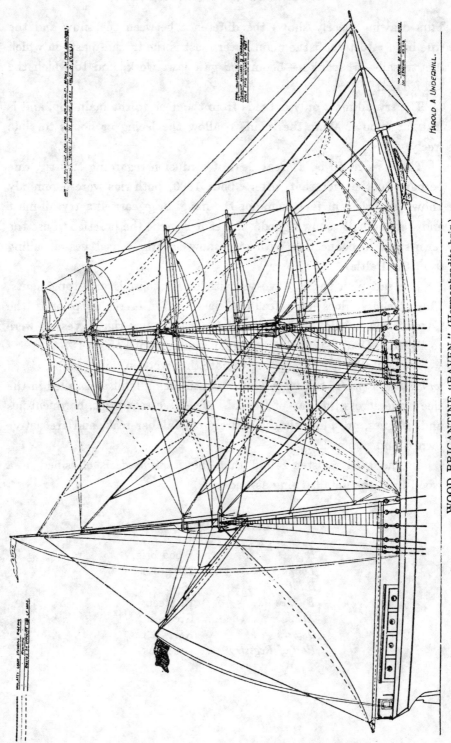

WOOD BRIGANTINE "RAVEN." (Hermaphrodite-brig.)

HAROLD A. UNDERHILL.

WOOD BRIGANTINE "RAVEN."

In calling the *Raven* a brigantine I am conforming to the modern practice; strictly speaking, this rig should be described as an hermaphrodite-brig. To be a true brigantine she should carry square topsails on the main topmast, as shown in the top sketch on page 7.

The Gulf of St. Lawrence is famous as the birthplace of many fine wooden vessels of all rigs, and is aptly described by F. W. Wallace as the home of "Wooden Ships and Iron Men." It was here that the *Raven* first entered the water, built by Keefe at Prince Edward Island in 1875. She later came to England under the ownership of J. C. Hoad of Rye.

This vessel must not be confused with the smaller brigantine—199 tons—of the same name, which was built by Duncan of Prince Edward Island in 1873. This last vessel was owned by J. G. Gann of Faversham, and remained on the register until 1916-17.

The *Raven* was a fine handy vessel, without any unusual or outstanding features, and she may be regarded as a typical example of the trading brigantine.

REGISTERED DETAILS.

Rig	Wood brigantine.
Tonnage	213 gross.
Built	1875.
By	Keefe, Prince Edward Island.
Owners	J. C. Hoad.
Port of Registry ..	Rye, Sussex.

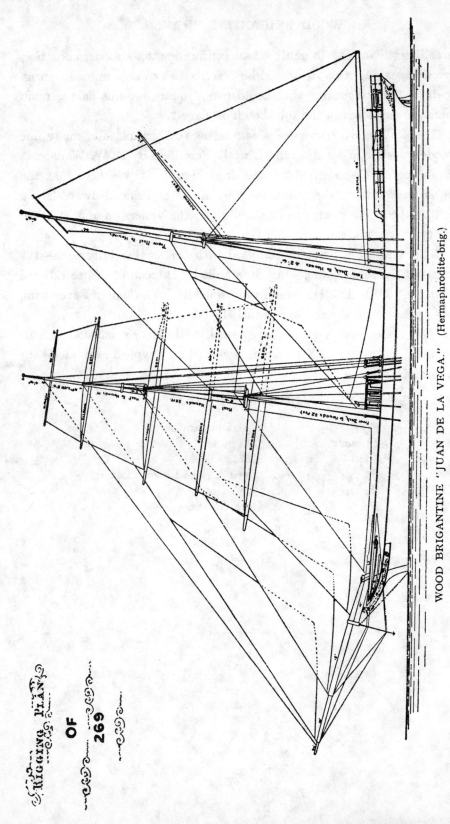

RIGGING PLAN

OF

269

WOOD BRIGANTINE "JUAN DE LA VEGA." (Hermaphrodite-brig.)

By permission of   Messrs. Alex. Hall & Co., Ltd., Aberdeen.

WOOD BRIGANTINE "JUAN DE LA VEGA."

ALTHOUGH I have very little information regarding this vessel, I feel sure that it will be of interest as an example of the work of a famous yard. What student of sailing ship history is not familiar with the name of Hall of Aberdeen?

The *Juan de la Vega* was launched at Aberdeen in 1871, and followed such ships as *Black Prince*, *Flying Spur*, etc., vessels which made Aberdeen's name in the China clipper period.

REGISTERED DETAILS.

Rig	Wood brigantine
Tonnage	172 net
Length	100·0 ft.
Breadth	24·0 ft.
Depth	12·3 ft.
Built	1871.
By	Hall at Aberdeen.
Owners	Vega-y-Veiga.
Port of Registry ..	Corunna.

AUXILIARY FOUR-MAST TOPSAIL SCHOONER "JUAN SEBASTIAN DE ELCANO."

HAROLD A. UNDERHILL.

By permission of Messrs. Camper & Nicholsons, Ltd., Southampton

AUXILIARY FOUR-MAST TOPSAIL SCHOONER
"JUAN SEBASTIAN DE ELCANO."

THE *Juan Sebastian de Elcano* is a steel auxiliary training vessel, built in 1927 for the Spanish Government.

Rigged as a four-mast topsail schooner, she has a generous sail plan of 28,000 sq. ft. in 19 sails. Her lower-masts, bowsprit, and lower yard are all of steel, while the topmasts and all other spars are Oregon pine.

Designed to provide sail and general training for naval officers and cadets, she has accommodation for a complement of 285, made up of 60 cadets, 57 officers, and 168 crew. She carries 12 boats in all, consisting of two motor lifeboats; four pulling lifeboats; one commander's launch; one officers' launch; one cutter; one cadets' gig, and two dinghies.

The auxiliary power is provided by a four-cylinder Diesel engine developing 800 b.h.p., which is sufficient to give her a speed of 9·5 knots under power alone. The exhaust from the motor is taken up the inside of the jigger lower-mast.

Her armament consists of four 6-pounder quick-firing guns, two mounted on the forecastle and two on the poop.

Although Spanish built, the *Juan Sebastian de Elcano* was designed by Mr. C. E. Nicholson of Messrs. Camper & Nicholsons, Ltd., Southampton, who was also responsible for all the working constructional drawings.

In later years the deckhouses between the fore and main rigging, and between the main and mizen, were extended out to the ship's side. This no doubt increased the accommodation, but by breaking up the sweep of the mainrail rather spoiled her general appearance.

GENERAL DETAILS.

Length overall	308 ft. 9 ins.
Length on waterline	260 ft. 0 ins.
Breadth moulded	43 ft. 0 ins.
Breadth extreme	43 ft. 2 ins.
Depth moulded (to upper deck)	28 ft. 6 ins.
Draught aft	21 ft. 6 ins.
Displacement	3220 tons.
Built	1927.
By	Messrs. Echevarrieta y Larrinaga.
At	Cadiz.

AUXILIARY TRAINING VESSEL "MERCATOR."
(Original Rig.)

By permission of

Messrs. G. L. Watson & Co., Glasgow.

AUXILIARY TRAINING VESSEL "MERCATOR."

THE *Mercator* is an auxiliary training vessel in the service of the Belgian Government. She was designed by Messrs. G. L. Watson & Co., of Glasgow, and built at Leith by Messrs. Ramage & Ferguson, Ltd.

The sail plan opposite shows the *Mercator* as originally designed and built, and it will be noticed that she was given the three-mast topsail schooner rig. This layout incorporates two rather unusual features, first the single square fore-topsail, and second the standing square fore-sail or fore-course. This rig gave her a sail area of some 18,200 square feet of canvas.

At a later date a fully square-rigged fore-mast, built up of three spars —lower-mast, topmast and topgallant mast, with the usual doublings— was fitted. Double-topsails were crossed in place of the original single topsail; the gaff foresail—or fore-spencer—was dispensed with and the usual staysails carried between the fore and main-masts, thus giving her the ordinary three-mast barquentine rig.

Her main and mizen gaff sails carry standing gaffs, the sails being brailed to the mast when furled, but the usual peak and throat halliards are rove so that the gaffs can come down for reefing.

During the Second World War she came under the British flag and served as a Navy Depot Ship in North Africa, but she returned to her normal training duties after the end of hostilities.

REGISTERED DETAILS.

Rig	Aux. Sc. three-mast barquentine.
Tonnage	770 gross.
Length	209·7 ft.
Breadth	35·0 ft.
Depth	16·8 ft.
Built	1932.
By	Ramage & Ferguson Ltd., Leith.
Owners	Belgian Government.
Port of Registry ..	Antwerp.
Flags	O S I A.

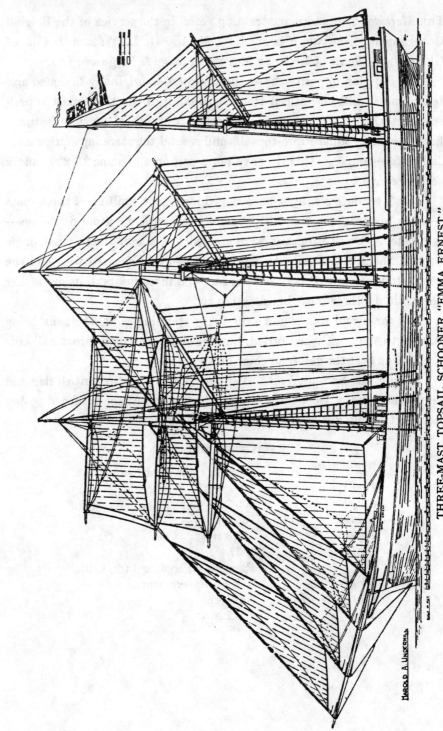

THREE-MAST TOPSAIL SCHOONER "EMMA ERNEST."

HAROLD A. UNDERHILL

THREE-MAST TOPSAIL SCHOONER "EMMA ERNEST."

THIS sail plan is typical of the many three-mast topsail schooners employed in the British coasting trade. Unfortunately the rig has now disappeared; either by being broken up, or by conversion into auxiliary fore-and-aft schooners with stumpy pole masts.

Although the *Emma Ernest* only carried two square sails, namely upper and lower fore-topsails, many of these vessels also crossed a small topgallant above this.

Like many other coasters she was built as a brig, then cut down to a barquentine, and later re-rigged as a three-mast topsail schooner. The sail plan opposite shows the latter rig, and I am indebted to Mr. Francis T. Wayne for his co-operation in producing it from measurements taken off the actual vessel.

At the end of her sea-going career she was bought by the Seven Seas Club and named *Friendship*, and she was still with us in 1937 moored off the Thames Embankment, and doing good service as a clubroom, although I believe that her name was changed to *Seven Seas*.

Her owners are to be congratulated on having made so few changes in her deck arrangement; in fact, except for converting her hatchways into skylights, they have left her much as she was in her coasting days.

It is a pity that her external paint work was not left in its original form, for she has been completely spoiled by the broad white band and row of small detached rectangles, which I suppose are intended to represent painted ports. She has also been given *square* (painted) hawsepipes! No wonder she seems to crouch under the bridge to hide her shame. However, long may she remain at her present moorings, a typical coasting schooner—in spite of her paint—in the very heart of London.

REGISTERED DETAILS.

Rig	Wood three-mast schooner.
Tonnage	191 gross.
Length	109·2 ft.
Breadth	23·7 ft.
Depth	12·5 ft.
Built	1876.
By	Jones, Milford.
Owner	A. Anderson.
Port of Registry ..	Faversham.
Flags	P N V F.

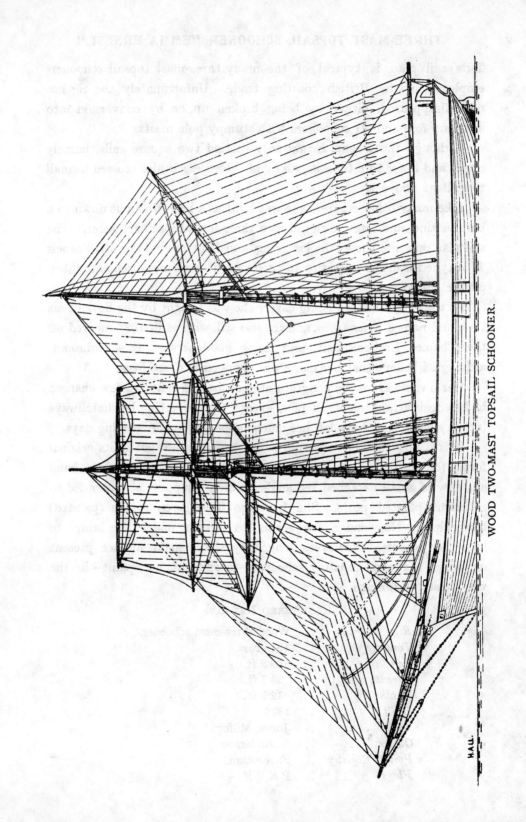

WOOD TWO-MAST TOPSAIL SCHOONER.

H.A.U.

TWO-MAST TOPSAIL SCHOONER.

THE sail plan opposite is based upon details taken from the schooner *Kate*, but as I did not have an opportunity of making a proper survey it is only put forward as a typical example and not as the sail plan of that particular vessel. However, except for minor details, all these schooners were very much alike.

One point of difference in this rig is the setting up of the fore topmast stay, or outer jib-stay. In some vessels this was set up to the fore crosstrees together with the fore-stay and jib-stay; others took it to a band on the topmast above the upper-topsail yard and just below the flying jib-stay; while a third arrangement was to take it to a band just above the lower-topsail yard, as shown in the frontispiece and plan opposite. This last method was perhaps the most used.

A feature of these vessels was the arrangement of the outer bobstay, as this lead seems to have been common only to the coasting fleet. As will be seen from the plan, the stay is composed of a running and a standing part, the latter is shackled to a chain plate on the stem at the waterline, and the former goes from the bowsprit end to a block on the standing part, back to a block on the bowsprit, thence to the deck where it is set up with lanyards.

Most of the later schooners carried the single spar standing bowsprit as shown, but at one time the bowsprit and jib-boom, with martingale and all the usual head gear, was most common.

One is apt to regard the coasting schooner as a bluff tubby little craft, but in many cases this was far from true, for there were some fine shapely hulls amongst the coasters. I have the half model of the schooner *Mary Ashburner* in my collection and I never tire of admiring her lines.

Some of the vessels were built for the fruit trade and made reputations as clippers; of course they had a more ample sail plan than in the plan opposite and were able to set stun'sails and other flying kites.

REGISTERED DETAILS OF "KATE."

Rig	..	..	Wood schooner.
Tonnage	..	..	129 gross.
Length	..	..	91·0 ft.
Breadth	..	..	22·0 ft.
Depth	..	..	11·3 ft.
Built	..	..	1872.
By ..	..	..	Graves, Isle of Man.
Owner	..	..	W. Thomas.
Port of Registry	..	Peel, Isle of Man.

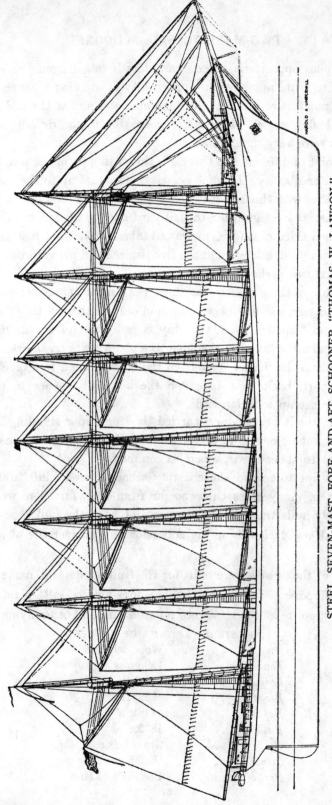

By permission of

STEEL SEVEN-MAST FORE-AND-AFT SCHOONER "THOMAS W. LAWSON."

The Bethlehem Shipbuilding Corp., Quincy, U.S.A

SEVEN-MAST FORE-AND-AFT SCHOONER "THOMAS W. LAWSON."

THIS was the only seven-mast schooner ever built, and was designed for the coasting trade of North America. The fore-and-aft rig has proved the most suitable for this service, and although the *Thomas W. Lawson* was the only vessel to be given seven masts, four and five-masters were very common.

She was built in 1902 by the Fore River Shipbuilding Company, at Quincy, Massachusetts, and with the exception of topmasts and spars, was constructed of steel throughout—a departure from the more common practice, as most of these vessels were built of wood. The seven masts were all of the same height, and consisted of a steel lower-mast 135 ft. from keel to cap, with a 58-ft. pine topmast above.

Steam power was provided for handling sail. A vertical steam boiler and winch was installed under the fo'castle, and to this the halliards, sheets and topping lifts of the forward sails were taken. A similar boiler and winch was carried in the after deckhouse, and handled the sails on the after masts.

The running gear of the lighter sails, such as topsail halliards, topsail sheets, etc., was taken to the four cargo winches amidships. Steam steering gear was also provided, her wheel being housed in a totally enclosed wheelhouse on the poop.

Thanks to all this steam equipment, this huge schooner of over 5000 tons was handled by sixteen men.

She made many coastal trips between Texas and Philadelphia, but was lost in 1907 when making a passage across the Atlantic. On December 13 she anchored off the Scilly Islands with the intention of riding out a gale, but during the night she capsized and except for one survivor all hands were lost.

REGISTERED DETAILS.

Rig	Seven-mast fore-and-aft schooner.
Tonnage	5218 gross.
Length overall ..	385 ft.
Length (waterline)	368 ft.
Breadth	50 ft.
Depth	35·2 ft. (to upper deck).
Built	1902.
By	Fore River Shipbuilding Co., Quincy, Mass., U.S.A.
Owners	Coastwise Transportation Co.
Port of Registry ..	Boston.

By permission of

THREE-MAST FORE-AND-AFT SCHOONER YACHT "SUNBEAM II."
(Original Rig).

Messrs. G. L. Watson & Co., Glasgow.

YACHT "SUNBEAM II."

THIS sail plan is an excellent example of the three-mast fore-and-aft schooner rig as applied to pleasure craft.

Sunbeam II. was designed by Messrs. G. L. Watson & Co. for Lord Runciman, and built on the Clyde by Messrs. Denny Bros., of Dumbarton.

She is an auxiliary vessel of 292 tons, built of steel, with steel lower-masts. Her topmasts and gaffs are hollow wood spars.

Although designed and completed as shown on the plan opposite, she was almost immediately re-rigged as a topsail schooner. This change was carried out by the addition of two yards on the fore-topmast, on which she set upper and lower square topsails, although the running square-sail on the lower yard was retained.

This alteration was made on the instructions of her owner, Lord Runciman, and brought her rig into line with that of the first *Sunbeam*, the steam-auxiliary yacht which became world famous under the owner-ship of Lord Brassey and later passed into the hands of Lord Runciman

In 1946 she was acquired by the Rydberg Foundation of Stockholm, and fitted out as a training ship to replace their four-masted barque *Abraham Rydberg*, which had been sold during the war. However after a few cruises she was laid up owing to lack of support.

In 1955 the Clipper Line of Malmo, Sweden, took her over, changing her name to *Flying Clipper* and putting her back into commission as a training ship, in which service she has made many cruises and taken part in the ocean races for sailing training ships.

Lloyds' have no rig classification for topsail schooners, so when she had the square yards added she became a "barquentine" in the Register, although she has of course always been a schooner.

REGISTERED DETAILS.

Rig	Aux. steel barquentine.
	[is in fact a topsail schooner]
Tonnage	292
Dimensions	
(Thames measurement)	167·0 ft. × 30·07 ft. × 17·6 ft.
Built	1929.
By	Denny Bros., Dumbarton.
Owner	Lord Runciman.
Port of Registration	London.
Flags	M P N K.

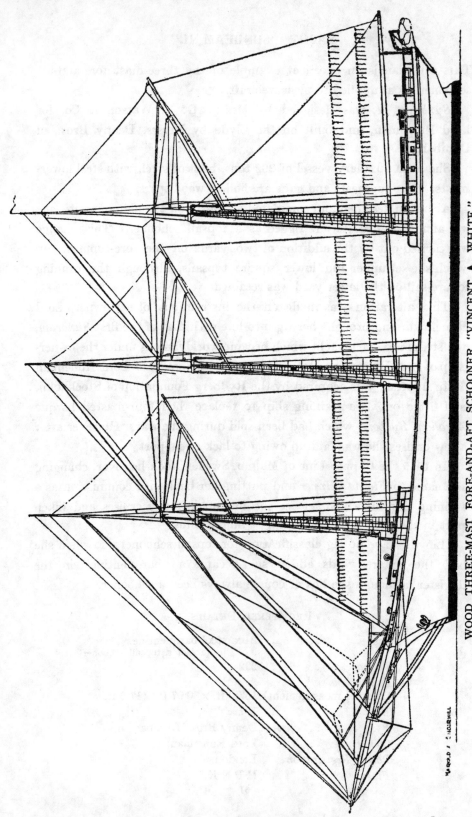

HAROLD J. UNDERHILL

WOOD THREE-MAST FORE-AND-AFT SCHOONER "VINCENT A. WHITE."

THREE-MAST FORE-AND-AFT SCHOONER "VINCENT A. WHITE."

THE *Vincent A. White* was a product of New Brunswick, so it is only natural that timber should be used for her construction. She is a typical vessel of that coast; the standing bowsprit and jib-boom, treble bobstay, and the booms on the fore-staysail and jib, all stamp her as belonging to the land of "Wooden Ships and Iron Men."

Her hull too is typical; the deck-house right forward with the fore-mast up through it; the raised quarter-deck with turned wood rails and boat in davits over the stern, and the modern stockless anchor at her bows.

She was built in 1918 and remained on the register until 1926-27, after which there is no further record and I have not been able to trace her fate.

This example of the three-mast fore-and-aft schooner rig in a trading vessel makes an interesting comparison with the yacht of the same rig on page 60.

REGISTERED DETAILS.

Rig	.. ..	Wood three-mast schooner.
Tonnage	.. ..	495 gross.
Length	.. ..	152·4 ft.
Breadth	.. ..	35·4 ft.
Depth	.. ..	12·8 ft.
Built	.. ..	1918.
By ..	.. ..	T. White & Son, Alma, N.B.
Port of Registry	..	Parrsborough.
Owners	.. ..	T. White & Son.

STEEL AUXILIARY THREE-MAST STAYSAIL SCHOONER "JOHN WILLIAMS V."

By permission of

Messrs. A. Goodwin-Hamilton & Adamson Ltd., Liverpool.

THREE-MAST STAYSAIL SCHOONER "JOHN WILLIAMS V."

THE *John Williams V* is an auxiliary steel schooner built for the London Missionary Society's Pacific Service. She was designed by Messrs. Goodwin-Hamilton & Adamson Ltd., of Liverpool, and built by the Grangemouth Dockyard Coy. Her sail plan, which provides an area of some 4000 sq. ft., is interesting and a distinct departure from the orthodox schooner, being more on the lines of the American staysail rig.

It may be of interest to recall the origin of her name. The Society have owned many vessels since their first ship, the full-rigged *Duff*—sailed from Britain on August 10, 1796—but none can be of greater interest than the schooner(?) *Messenger of Peace*, built by Rev. John Williams on the island of Rarotonga in 1827, the whole work being finished in fifteen weeks.

The timber was cut in the bush, and as no suitable saw was available it was split to size by means of wedges. The rest of the material used was improvised as follows: all fastenings, wood pegs, as metal not available; for oakum, cocoa-nut fibre; for ropes, the bark of the hibiscus; for sails, small native mats sewn together; rudder pintles from a pick-axe, a cooper's adze and a garden hoe; masts and spars, from poles with hardly 6 feet of straight in them. The builder says that she was not quite the same on both sides, and sailed better on one tack than another, which is not surprising under the circumstances! One would like to know a little more about her pumps, but the only information available is that they were "contrived with great mechanical ingenuity."

Her first passage was to Aitutaki—340 miles the round trip—where, to quote contemporary reports, "her strange uncanny build and rig caused immense excitement." Small wonder! After this she made regular passages of 600 to 700 miles, and with a proper set of spars fitted she remained in commission until 1833 when she was *sold*! After such an achievement it is not strange that the Society have named all subsequent vessels *John Williams*.

REGISTERED DETAILS.

Rig	Aux. steel three-mast schooner.
Tonnage	227 gross.
Length	117·6 ft.
Breadth	25·1 ft.
Depth (of hold) ..	8·5 ft.
Built	1930.
By	Grangemouth Dockyard Co., Ltd.
Owners	London Missionary Society.
Port of Registry ..	London.
Flags ..	M P S Z.

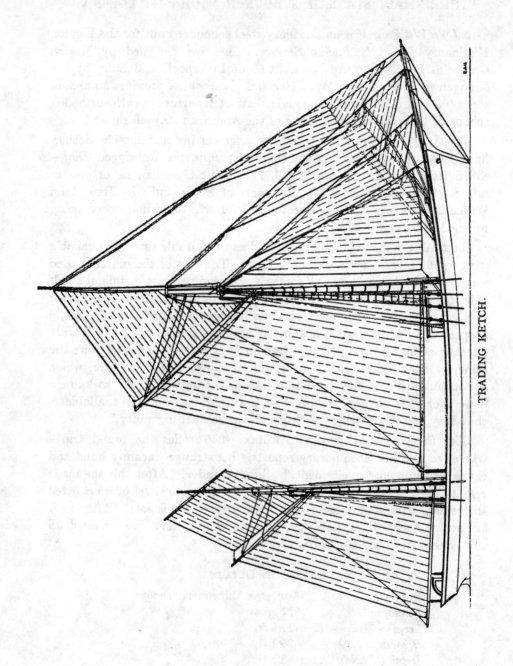

TRADING KETCH.

TRADING KETCH.

Up to the second world war, one could always find a ketch-rigged coaster in almost any of the creeks, or smaller ports round the coast, either alongside some old quay, or discharging direct into carts as she lay high and dry at low tide. To-day only one or two are left, and I am afraid that a few more years will see the end of another link with the days of sail.

Most of these sea-going trading ketches had standing bowsprits, and in one or two cases bowsprit and jib-boom, while the arrangement of the head-sails and gear followed that of their larger sister the schooner. Many ketches carried a yard on the main, on which a square-sail was set when running.

Like most of the wooden coasters they were sturdy, well built craft and it is interesting to recall that one of these vessels was built in the time of Napoleon and remained in active commission until November 1936, when she was lost at the age of *one hundred and twenty-three years*. This was the *Ceres* of Bude, Cornwall, a well-known craft on the South Coast.

Ceres was built as a cutter, but at the age of 63 years she was lengthened by 15 ft., being cut in two, the two sections drawn apart and a new mid-body built between them. On completion a new mizen mast was stepped, so converting her into a ketch. When about 103 years of age she was given an auxiliary engine, but still retaining her ketch rig.

The sail plan on the opposite page is typical of the trading ketch and was compiled from an old builders' plan dated 1880; it illustrates a vessel of the following dimensions.

Length	.. ..	87·5 ft.
Breadth	.. ..	22·0 ft.
Depth	.. ..	9·5 ft.
Tonnage	.. ..	95 tons gross.

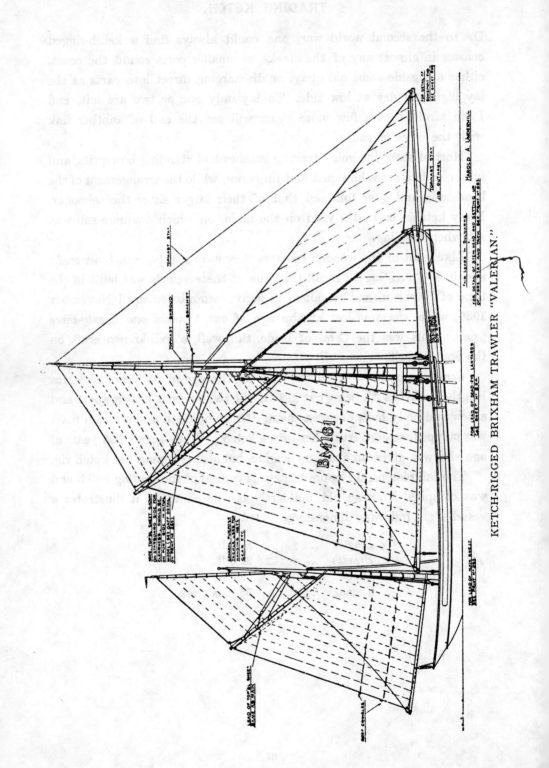

KETCH-RIGGED BRIXHAM TRAWLER "VALERIAN."

HAROLD A. UNDERHILL

BRIXHAM TRAWLER "VALERIAN."

THE fishing craft is perhaps the best known example of the ketch rig, and up to the First World War large fleets of them could be seen at such ports as Brixham, Grimsby, Lowestoft, etc., but the steam trawler and auxiliary boats have taken the place of the sailing craft.

The fishing ketch differed from the trading vessel of the same rig by having a running bowsprit, and her jib set flying instead of being hanked to a stay. Further, she only set two head-sails, except perhaps when racing in the annual regatta, for which she may have set a balloon-jib on the topmast-stay.

In a general sense the rig remained the same all round the coast, although actually each locality had its own little individualities in rig, cut of sails, or run of gear. The drawing opposite shows a Brixham boat in her summer rig; during the winter a main-topmast some 12 ft. shorter was used.

These Brixham boats were very fine vessels, and it used to be a magnificent sight to see the whole fleet putting to sea after the week-end in harbour. I have not been to Brixham for many years, but I understand that there are not many, if any, of the old boats left now.

The principal dimensions of the *Valerian* are :—

Length overall	.. ..	78 ft. 10 ins.
Beam	.. .. ..	18 ft. 7 ins.
Draught	.. ..	9 ft. 7 ins.
Main-mast (deck to cap)		46 ft. 9 ins.
Topmast	.. .. ..	37 ft. 6 ins.
Mizen (deck to truck)	..	43 ft. 6 ins.
Bowsprit (outboard)	..	24 ft. 9 ins.

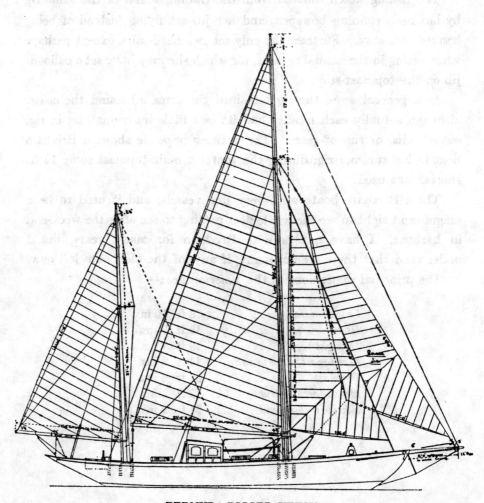

BERMUDA-RIGGED KETCH.

By permission of   Messrs. G. L. Watson & Co., Glasgow

BERMUDA KETCH.

THE yacht on the opposite page is a good illustration of a modern Bermuda-rigged ketch.

She is an auxiliary vessel, being fitted with a paraffin motor. Her principal dimensions are as under:

(Thames measurement)		48·6 ft. × 12·7 ft. × 8·2 ft.
Length overall	.. ..	56·5 ft.
Length on waterline	..	41·0 ft.
Draft	.. .. ..	7·7 ft.
Tonnage	.. ..	31 tons reg.
Sail area	.. ..	1400 square ft.

She was built of wood in 1937.

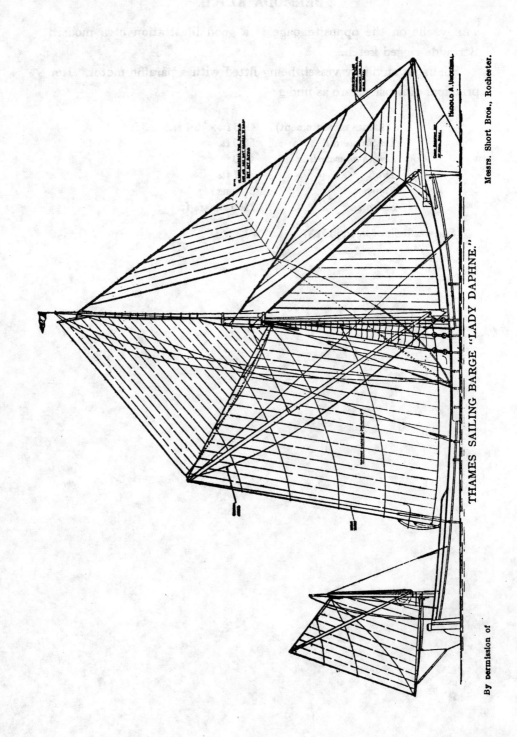

THAMES SAILING BARGE "LADY DAPHNE."

By permission of   Messrs. Short Bros., Rochester.

THAMES BARGE "LADY DAPHNE."

THE word barge rather suggests a dirty grubby craft, but there is nothing of that nature about the Thames sailing barge. Essentially a seaworthy and handy vessel, she is the largest sailing craft in the world to be handled by two men. The average size is about 120 tons, with a sail area of some 4200 square feet in six working sails. No other rig of this size could be managed by such a small crew, but the main-sail, being set up by a sprit, remains aloft, and when taking this sail in it is simply brailed, or gathered, in to the mast. The topsail also remains aloft, and is controlled from the deck by halliards, in-haul, sheets, etc. Both main and fore-sheets work on horses across the deck and do not require to be handed when going about. The mizen sheet leads down on to the rudder, and by forcing the boom to windward when the helm is put down, assists in bringing her up into the wind.

The masts are fitted in tabernacles and can be lowered with all gear set, being rehoisted by means of a heavy purchase on the fore-stay. Unlike most other vessels, the barge uses her topsail as one of her principal working sails, and it is quite common for them to use topsail and head-sails only when making a passage in heavy weather. In the upper reaches of the river they could be seen dodging in and out, with bowsprits canted up and the fore-topmast staysail—or spinnaker as the bargemen call it—set up to the stem-head, although they have now almost completely disappeared.

The Thames barge is capable of making long passages, and could be seen as far afield as the Bristol Channel and Continental ports. Some years ago the *Lady Daphne* made a name for herself by sailing unaided from the Lizard to the Scillies. She was abandoned by her crew when off the Lizard in a gale of wind; later she was sighted by a steamer, but was holding her course so well that the master had no idea that he was missing a chance for salvage. As she approached St. Mary's, people ashore remarked how well she was being handled, and it was only when she ran ashore at the entrance to the roadstead that it became apparent that something was wrong. She was salved and is still in commission, although a year or so ago she was converted into an auxiliary.

REGISTERED DETAILS.

Rig	..	.. Spritsail barge.
Tonnage	..	.. 116 net.
Built	..	.. 1923.
By ..	..	.. Short Bros., Rochester.
Owners	..	.. L. Bradley.
Port of Registry	..	Rochester.

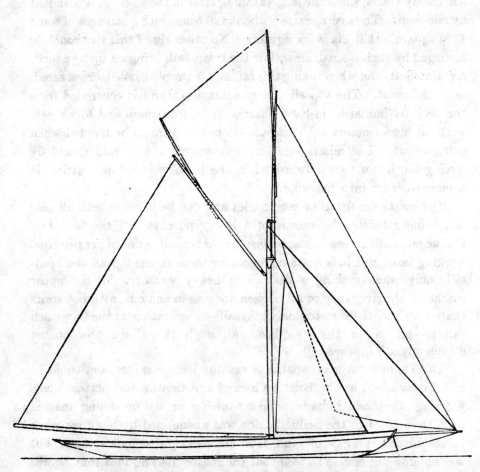

H.M. YACHT "BRITANNIA." Original Sail Plan of 1893.

By permission of   Messrs. G. L. Watson & Co., Glasgow.

CUTTER YACHT "BRITANNIA."

IT would be difficult to find a vessel having a greater hold on the general public than the *Britannia* had; this was not confined to yachtsmen and ship lovers, but seemed to cover all walks of life. I suppose the fact that right up to the end she was able to compete with, and win prizes from, crack vessels built almost half a century after her launch, caught the popular fancy and endeared her to many who otherwise had no interest in either ships or the sea. After all it *was* something to be proud of; how many other vessels of her type could claim some forty years of active service and successful racing?

The *Britannia* was built in 1893 for King Edward VII.—then Prince of Wales—to the design of the late Mr. G. L. Watson; the builders being Messrs. D. & W. Henderson, Glasgow. She was of composite construction, 221 tons Thames measurement, on a waterline of 87·8 ft.

In hull design she was a complete departure from the racing craft of her period, these being of the deep "plank on edge" type, while the *Britannia* was intended to skim the surface of the water rather than drive through it. When she first came out her bow received much adverse criticism, as at that time most of the racing vessels had the clipper or swan bow, and the *Britannia's* stem was thought to be very unsightly. However she was not long in proving her worth, and by the end of her first season's racing she had 20 first prizes to her credit, while the yacht with the next highest total had 11.

During her long racing career the sail plan of the *Britannia* was altered and modernised several times, and I am indebted to Messrs. G. L. Watson & Co. for details of these alterations and permission to reproduce the two sails plans included in this work. The plan on page 74 shows the original gaff cutter rig of 1893, while that on page 76 is the final Bermuda rig. This latter rig may have many advantages, but I am afraid that beauty cannot be said to be one of them!

The first alteration was to shorten all her spars, giving her a reduced sail area, as at that time it was intended to convert her for cruising purposes.

In 1920-1 she was again given a racing rig and a new head was built on to her lower-mast, making it some 10 ft. longer than it was when first put into her in 1893; this gave her a more lofty sail plan.

In 1927 the sail plan was again raised, and a new topmast fitted. This new mast was socketed into the head of the lower-mast, converting

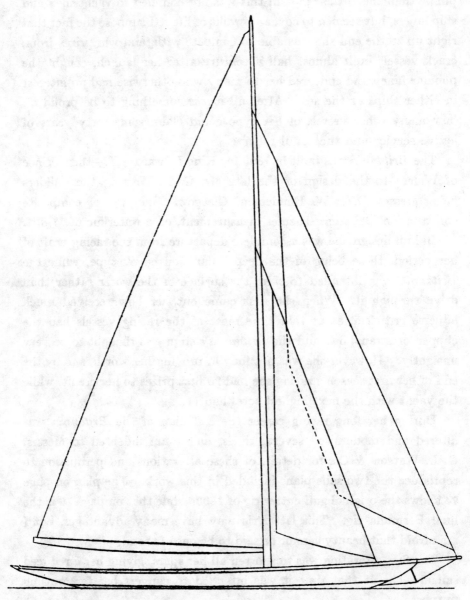

H.M. YACHT "BRITANNIA."   Last Bermuda Sail Plan.

it into a single spar in place of the old fidded topmast with the usual doubling.   With this new rig she still retained the jackyard topsail.

The next change came in 1928 when she was given a full "Marconi" mast so that the luff of the topsail hoisted on the mast without any need for a yard.   All this time she retained her gaff cutter rig.

The final alteration was to the Bermuda rig shown on the opposite page.

It is interesting to note that in 1932 His late Majesty King George V presented the mast removed from the *Britannia* to the Royal Alfred Aged Merchant Seamen's Institution, and it is now in use at their Belvedere home as a flagstaff.   The first flag to be flown from this mast in its new position was broken out by H.R.H. the Duke of Kent.

It is not generally realised that the *Britannia* changed hands eight or nine times during her career.   She was, as already stated, built in 1893 for King Edward, then Prince of Wales.   In 1897 she was sold and passed to several owners until being repurchased by the Prince of Wales in 1899.   She was again sold in 1900, only to be repurchased by King Edward in 1902.   From that time she remained under Royal ownership until 1936, when after the death of His Majesty King George V she was towed to sea and sunk.   A fitting end for a fine vessel.

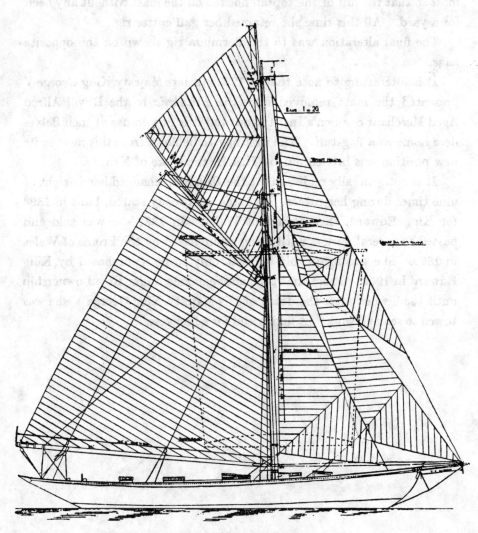

GAFF-RIGGED CUTTER.

By permission of   Messrs. G. L. Watson & Co., Glasgow.

GAFF CUTTER.

THE drawing opposite shows the sail plan of a fine modern gaff-rigged cutter-yacht, built in 1929.

I suppose that I am old fashioned and out of date, but I must admit that I find beauty in this little ship, beauty which I cannot see in the modern Bermuda rig.

I have no doubt that there is much to be said for the present day triangular sail plan, but for good looks give me the gaff rig every time. Compare the *Britannia's* 1893 sail plan on page 74 with the Bermuda rig on page 76, or perhaps I should have said *can* you compare these two rigs!

The cutter opposite is built of wood and fitted with an auxiliary petrol motor, and her principal dimensions are as under:—

(Thames measurement)		58·5×14·0×9·1 ft.
Length overall ..	..	67·0 ft.
Length waterline	..	50·0 ft.
Draft	..	7·9 ft.
Tonnage	..	28·06.
Sail area ..	..	1800 square feet.

SAILING LIFE-BOAT.

Messrs. G. L. Watson & Co., Consulting Naval Architects to the Royal National Life-boat Institution

By permission of

SAILING LIFE-BOAT.

THE work of vessels belonging to the Royal National Life-boat Institution is too well known to call for any comment, and I am very pleased to be able to include one of their boats in this collection of sail and rigging plans.

The boat on the opposite page is a Watson sailing life-boat, designed by the late Mr. G. L. Watson, the designer of the *Britannia*, and is a typical example of the type of boat at one time used on stations from which it was often necessary to go well out to sea.

The rig consists of two standing lugs and a single head-sail. The principal aim in designing these boats was to provide the best possible sea-going qualities, and in this the designer was most successful. They proved to be safe weatherly craft, quick in stays and having a good turn of speed.

By the time these boats were designed it had been proved that for certain types, seaworthiness and speed were of greater importance than self-righting, and it will be noticed that the end air compartments—or end-boxes, which are always a feature of the self-righting boat—are much smaller and less conspicuous.

In hull form the sailing life-boat had greater beam and less sheer than the self-righting or pulling boat, but her lines were finer, with a greater rise of floor and sharper end sections.

The full powered life-boat has taken the place of the pulling and sailing boats round our coast, and so marks another epoch in the history of sail.

I am indebted to Messrs. G. L. Watson & Co. for the trouble they have taken in turning up Mr. Watson's original design and their permission to reproduce it here.

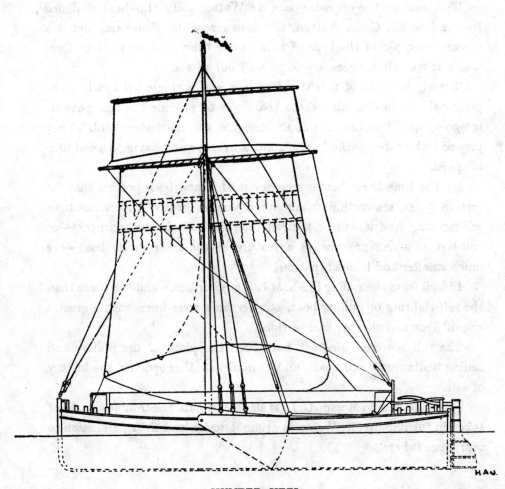

HUMBER KEEL.

HUMBER KEEL.

THE Humber keel was a barge used on the Yorkshire waterways. She was a strongly built, double-ended craft, with almost square ends, and so bluff are the bow and stern that a 60 ft. keel reached maximum width of beam within 5 ft. 6 ins of stem and stern posts. Her sides were parallel, and her midship section full with flat floors. Below the waterline the after body was finer than the bow, otherwise the rudder would be operating in dead water.

The deck plan of a keel was almost all hatch; she had a short deck at each end, connected on either side by narrow gangways outside the hatch coamings. On the fore-deck was an old type windlass; simply a barrel with a pawl in the centre and holes at each end for hand-spikes. On the after deck was a water butt and companion to a small cabin below.

A feature of these craft was the arrangement of the timber heads at bow and stern; these projected up through the deck for a foot or so and were then cut off without any attempt to form a terminal. A heavy rail ran round the stern, and on this were small hand winches to operate the leeboards. The deadweight carrying capacity of a standard keel was about 100 tons.

The sail plan was a thing apart and does not come under any standard classification, but was rather reminiscent of the thirteenth century. It consisted of a pole mast, fitted in a tabernacle so that it could be lowered when negotiating bridges; on this was set a square-sail and topsail. The lower, or main-sail, had two rows of reef points and the usual tacks and sheets, while on the fore side was a single buntline and span. A single brace led from each lower yardarm to a belaying post at the tiller. No braces were fitted to the topsail. When close-hauled a bowline was led from the weather leech to a block on the fore-stay, and so to the deck.

The topsail was set flying, and when not required was taken in complete with yard. All gear was taken aft to near the tiller, which, with the aid of small hand winches, enabled a man and his wife to handle the vessel. The keel shown on the opposite page is 61·0 ft. long with a beam of 15·5 ft.

SECTION III.
Diagrams, Tables and Notes.

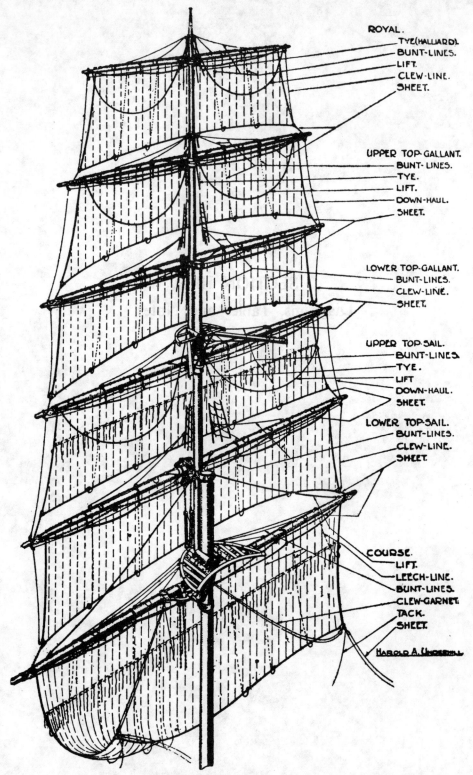

ROYAL.
TYE (HALLIARD).
BUNT-LINES.
LIFT.
CLEW-LINE.
SHEET.

UPPER TOP-GALLANT.
BUNT-LINES.
TYE.
LIFT.
DOWN-HAUL.
SHEET.

LOWER TOP-GALLANT.
BUNT-LINES.
CLEW-LINE.
SHEET.

UPPER TOP-SAIL.
BUNT-LINES
TYE.
LIFT
DOWN-HAUL.
SHEET.

LOWER TOP-SAIL.
BUNT-LINES.
CLEW-LINE.
SHEET.

COURSE.
LIFT.
LEECH-LINE.
BUNT-LINES.
CLEW-GARNET.
TACK.
SHEET.

HAROLD A. UNDERHILL

PERSPECTIVE DRAWING OF MODERN SQUARE-RIGGED MAST.
Showing sails set and lead of running rigging.

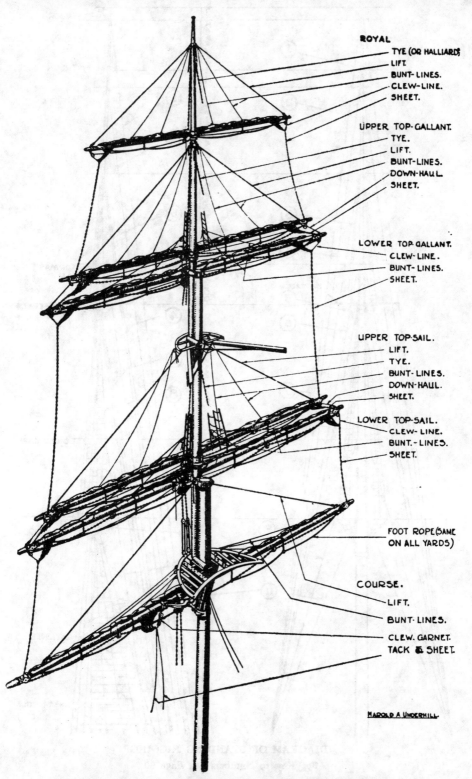

ROYAL
    TYE (OR HALLIARD)
    LIFT.
    BUNT-LINES.
    CLEW-LINE.
    SHEET.

UPPER TOP-GALLANT.
    TYE.
    LIFT.
    BUNT-LINES.
    DOWN-HAUL
    SHEET.

LOWER TOP-GALLANT.
    CLEW-LINE.
    BUNT-LINES.
    SHEET.

UPPER TOP-SAIL.
    LIFT.
    TYE.
    BUNT-LINES.
    DOWN-HAUL.
    SHEET.

LOWER TOP-SAIL.
    CLEW-LINE.
    BUNT.-LINES.
    SHEET.

FOOT ROPE (SAME ON ALL YARDS)

COURSE.
    LIFT.
    BUNT-LINES.
    CLEW. GARNET.
    TACK & SHEET.

HAROLD A UNDERHILL

PERSPECTIVE DRAWING OF MODERN SQUARE-RIGGED MAST.

This drawing shows the same mast as opposite page but indicates the
position of yards and running rigging when sails are furled.

85

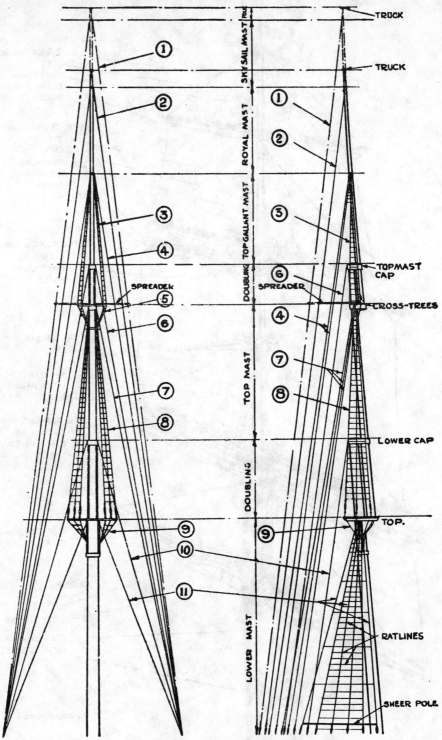

DIAGRAM OF STANDING RIGGING.
For Key to Numbers See Page 90

DESCRIPTION OF SQUARE SAILS.

THOSE not familiar with the different combinations of square sails may find it difficult to distinguish between the various arrangements; for instance, a vessel with royals over single topgallants has the same number of yards as a vessel stump-topgallant rigged, yet the rigs are quite distinct. It is to help the young student of sailing ship construction over this difficulty that the diagrams on pages 88 and 91 have been included.

The first principle is that a sailing ship's mast is built up, or divided, into a number of sections, *i.e.* lower-mast; topmast; topgallant-mast; royal-mast; and in some cases a skysail-mast above this. This construction will be understood from the diagram on page 86.

The second principle is that all square sails—with the exception of those on the lower-masts—take their names from the section of the mast upon which they are carried. Thus a sail on the topmast is a topsail; on the topgallant-mast a topgallant; on the royal-mast a royal; and on the skysail-mast a skysail. The only exception to this is the sail on the lower-mast, which, on the fore lower-mast is a foresail; on the main lower-mast a main-sail; and on the mizen lower-mast a cross-jack, or cro'jack. Collectively these lower sails are known as courses.

In the early days when large crews were carried, all ships were rigged with what is known as single topsails and topgallants, as illustrated in Fig. 1 on page 88. From this diagram it will be seen that each sail extends to the full height of the particular mast to which it belongs. This is the single topsail rig, and the sail plan of the *Runnymede* on page 44 shows an example of this.

By about 1853 crews were being reduced in number, and single topsails were rather large for the smaller crews to handle, so the sail was divided into two smaller sails, *i.e.* upper and lower topsails. This rig, Fig. 3, which has single topgallants and royals—and sometimes skysails—over double-topsails is perhaps the most common one, and plenty of examples will be found among the sail plans in this book. Both the *Loch Etive* and *Coriolanus* belong to this rig.

By 1870 when ships were getting larger, and incidentally crews smaller in number, it was found necessary to divide the topgallants

87

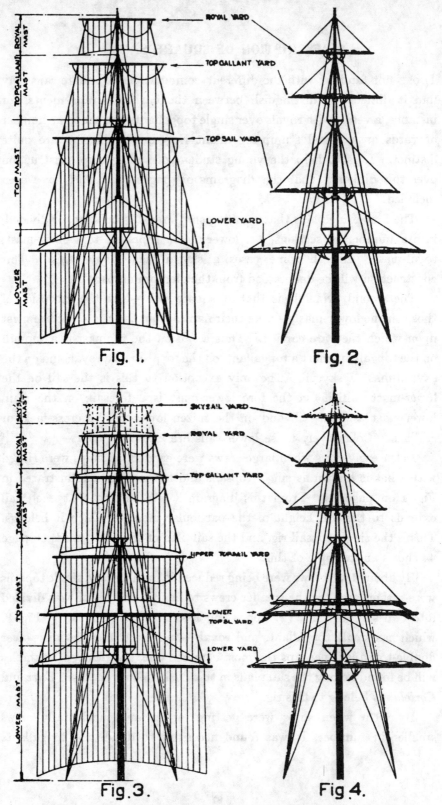

Fig. 1.

Fig. 2.

Fig. 3.

Fig 4.

ROYAL YARD

TOP GALLANT YARD

TOP SAIL YARD

LOWER YARD

SKYSAIL YARD

ROYAL YARD

TOP GALLANT YARD

UPPER TOPSAIL YARD

LOWER TOPS'L YARD

LOWER YARD

ROYAL MAST

TOPGALLANT MAST

TOP MAST

LOWER MAST

SKY'S'L MAST

ROYAL MAST

TOPGALLANT MAST

TOP MAST

LOWER MAST

DIAGRAMS OF DIFFERENT RIGS SHOWING POSITION OF YARDS
WITH SAILS SET AND FURLED.

too, as indicated in Fig. 5. This is the double-topsail and double-topgallant rig, and has royals above the topgallants. Most modern vessels were so rigged and actual examples will be found in the sail plans of the *Preussen, Potosi, Acamas,* and others.

It will be understood that skysails can be carried above any of the rigs already described, although double-topgallants came in about the time that sailing ships were being reduced in height and given greater spread.

Lastly comes the stump-topgallant, or baldheaded rig (Fig. 7). This only came in at the end of the sailing ship era, a time when every effort was being made to run ships as cheaply as possible. Further, by this time speed as far as the sailing ship was concerned was no longer an important factor: the main thing was to carry as much as possible at the minimum cost. To enable the number of hands to be still further reduced, all lighter sails were dispensed with, and no sail carried above the upper-topgallant. This is the stump-topgallant or baldheaded rig. Both the *Pommern* on page 32 and *Mozart* on page 38 are stump-topgallant rigged.

It will perhaps be as well to explain just what happens to the yards when the sails are furled, as this seems to be rather a snare to some ship model builders. The other day I saw a model which for workmanship was perfect, but completely spoiled by having sails set and the upper-topsail and upper-topgallant yards *down*. After discreet enquiries, I found that the rigging had been copied from a photograph of the ship with sails furled, and the model maker had thought the upper-topsail and upper-topgallant yards were booms to spread the foot of the sail above! This gave him four sails on six yards.

On the right of each sail diagram I have included one showing the same mast with sails furled. Thus Fig. 2 indicates the new position of the yards on the mast in Fig. 1. It will be clear that the topsail yard is lowered until it rests on the lower-cap; the topgallant yard on to the topmast-cap; the royal yard to the head of the topgallant rigging; and the skysail—when carried—to the head of the royal rigging. The lower yard always remains in one position.

Fig. 4 shows the double-topsail rig. It will be seen that the lower-topsail yard is attached to the lower cap, and the upper-topsail yard is lowered on to it. All the other sails are taken in as described for Fig. 2.

Fig. 6 shows double-topgallants over double-topsails. The lower-topgallant yard is attached to the topmast-cap and remains in position, while the upper-topgallant yard is lowered on to it. The remainder of the sails are handled as described for Fig. 4. The perspective drawings on pages 84 and 85 illustrate this rig, and also include the running gear.

Fig. 8 shows the stump-topgallant rig, which is the same as the foregoing, except that there are no sails above the upper-topgallants.

It will be seen from these diagrams that, broadly speaking, the courses, lower-topsails, and lower-topgallants are all clewed *up* to their respective yards. The upper-topsails and upper-topgallants are *lowered*—together with their yards—on to the yards below. While the royals—and skysails when carried—both clew up and the yards come down. A study of the perspective drawings on pages 84 and 85 will help in understanding this. The standing rigging has been omitted from these drawings so that the lead of the running gear may be followed.

Sails are always furled along the *top* of their respective yards.

KEY TO STANDING RIGGING DIAGRAM ON PAGE 86.

1. Skysail-backstay.
2. Royal-backstay.
3. Topgallant-rigging or shrouds.
4. Topgallant-backstays.
5. Topgallant-futtock-shrouds.
6. Topmast-capstay.
7. Topmast-backstays.
8. Topmast-rigging or shrouds.
9. Lower-futtock-shrouds.
10. Lower-capstay.
11. Lower-rigging or shrouds.

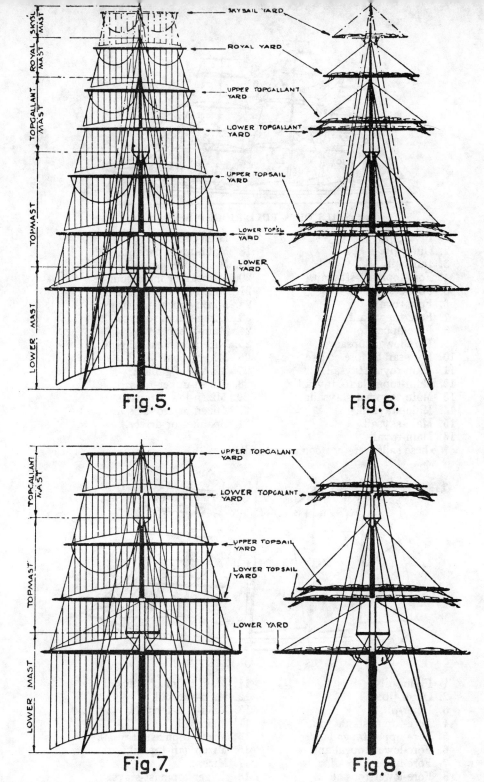

SKYSAIL YARD

ROYAL YARD

UPPER TOPGALLANT YARD

LOWER TOPGALLANT YARD

UPPER TOPSAIL YARD

LOWER TOPS'L YARD

LOWER YARD

SKYSL MAST

ROYAL MAST

TOPGALLANT MAST

TOPMAST

LOWER MAST

Fig. 5.

Fig. 6.

UPPER TOPGALANT YARD

LOWER TOPGALLANT YARD

UPPER TOPSAIL YARD

LOWER TOPSAIL YARD

LOWER YARD

TOPGALLANT MAST

TOPMAST

LOWER MAST

Fig. 7.

Fig. 8.

DIAGRAMS OF DIFFERENT RIGS SHOWING POSITION OF YARDS
WITH SAILS SET AND FURLED.

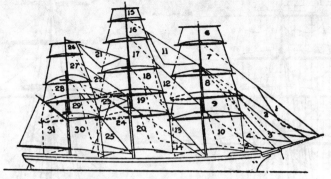

SAILS OF A FULL-RIGGED SHIP.

1. Flying-jib.	17. Main-topgallant.
2. Outer-jib.	18. Main-upper-topsail.
3. Inner-jib.	19. Main-lower-topsail.
4. Fore-topmast-staysail.	20. Mainsail or main-course.
5. Fore-staysail.*	21. Mizen-royal-staysail.
6. Fore-royal.	22. Mizen-topgallant-staysail.
7. Fore-topgallant.	23. Mizen-middle-staysail.*
8. Fore-upper-topsail.	24. Main-spencer.*
9. Fore-lower-topsail.	25. Mizen-topmast-staysail.
10. Fore-sail or fore-course.	26. Mizen-royal.
11. Main-royal-staysail.	27. Mizen-topgallant.
12. Main-topgallant-staysail.	28. Mizen-upper-topsail.
13. Main topmast-staysail.	29. Mizen-lower-topsail.
14. Main-staysail.*	30. Mizen or cro'jack.
15. Main-skysail.	31. Spanker or driver.
16. Main-royal.	

* These sails were not common to all ships.

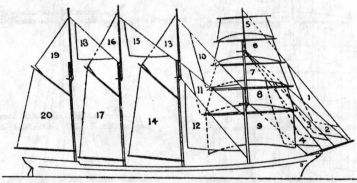

SAILS OF A BARQUENTINE.

1. Flying-jib.	11. Main-topmast-staysail.
2. Outer-jib.	12. Main-staysail.
3. Inner-jib.	13. Main-gaff-topsail.
4. Fore-topmast-staysail.	14. Main-sail.
5. Fore-upper-topgallant.	15. Mizen-topmast-staysail.
6. Fore-lower-topgallant.	16. Mizen-gaff-topsail.
7. Fore-upper-topsail.	17. Mizen.
8. Fore-lower-topsail.	18. Jigger-topmast-staysail.
9. Fore-sail or fore-course.	19. Jigger-gaff topsail.
10. Main-topgallant-staysail.	20. Jigger or spanker.

NOTE.—This diagram shows a barquentine with stump-topgallant rig on the fore-mast, but a barquentine can carry royals and skysails on the fore.

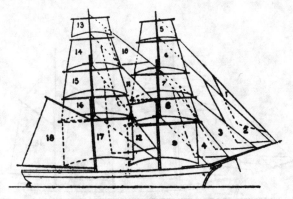

SAILS OF A BRIG OR SNOW.

1. Flying-jib.
2. Fore-topgallant-staysail or outer-jib.
3. Jib.
4. Fore-topmast-staysail.
5. Fore-royal.
6. Fore-topgallant.
7. Fore-upper-topsail.
8. Fore-lower-topsail.
9. Fore-sail or fore-course.
10. Main-royal-staysail.
11. Main-topgallant-staysail.
12. Main-topmast-staysail.
13. Main-royal.
14. Main-topgallant.
15. Main-upper-topsail.
16. Main-lower-topsail.
17. Main-sail or main course.
18. Spanker, driver or trysail

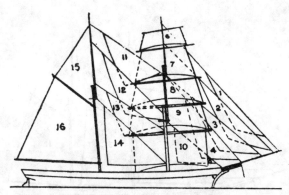

SAILS OF A BRIGANTINE. (Hermaphrodite-brig.)

1. Flying-jib.
2. Fore-topgallant-staysail or outer-jib.
3. Jib.
4. Fore-topmast-staysail.
5. Fore-staysail.*
6. Fore-royal.
7. Fore-topgallant.
8. Fore-upper-topsail.
9. Fore-lower-topsail.
10. Fore-sail or fore-course.
11. Main-topgallant-staysail.
12. Main-topmast-staysail.
13. Middle-staysail.
14. Main-staysail.
15. Gaff-topsail.
16. Main-sail, spanker or driver.

* This sail was not in general use.

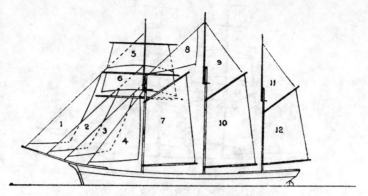

SAILS OF A TOPSAIL SCHOONER.

1. Flying-jib.
2. Fore-topmast-staysail or outer-
   jib.
3. Jib.
4. Fore-staysail.
5. Fore-upper-topsail.
6. Fore-lower-topsail.

7. Fore-sail.
8. Main-topmast-staysail.
9. Main-gaff-topsail.
10. Main-sail.
11. Mizen-gaff-topsail.
12. Mizen.

NOTE.—The sails of a two-mast topsail schooner are as above but Nos. 11 and 12 are omitted.

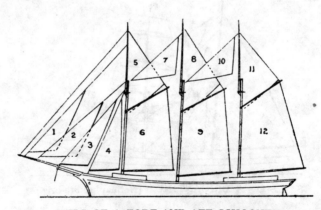

SAILS OF A FORE-AND-AFT SCHOONER.

1. Flying-jib.
2. Fore-topmast-staysail or outer-
   jib.
3. Jib.
4. Fore-staysail.
5. Fore-gaff-topsail.
6. Fore-sail.

7. Main-topmast-staysail.
8. Main-gaff-topsail.
9. Main-sail.
10. Mizen-topmast-staysail.
11. Mizen-gaff-topsail.
12. Mizen.

NOTE.—The names of a two-mast schooner are as above but Nos. 10, 11 and 12 are omitted.

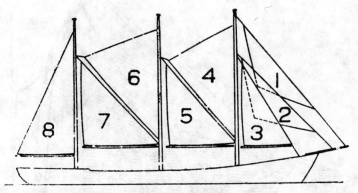

SAILS OF A STAYSAIL SCHOONER.

1. Flying-jib or outer-jib.
2. Jib.
3. Fore-staysail.
4. Fore-trysail.
5. Main-staysail
6. Main-trysail.
7. Mizen-staysail.
8. Jib-headed-spanker.

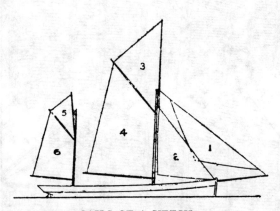

SAILS OF A KETCH.

1. Jib.
2. Fore-sail or fore-staysail
3. Main-topsail.
4. Main-sail.
5. Mizen-topsail.
6. Mizen.

95

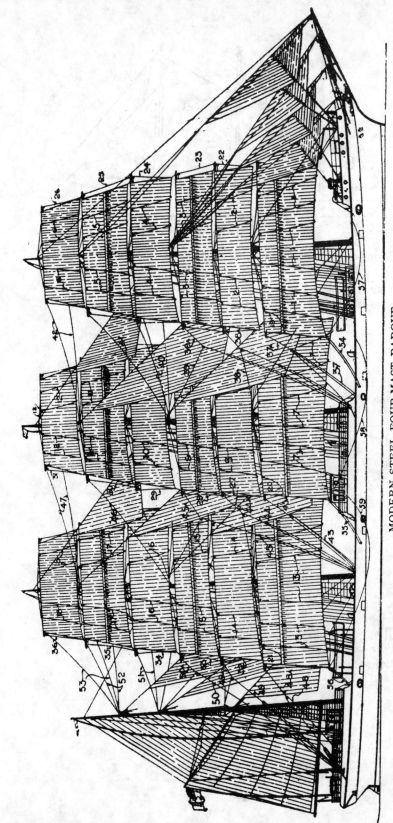

MODERN STEEL FOUR-MAST BARQUE.

Diagram of running rigging on fore-side of sails.

RUNNING RIGGING ON FORE-SIDE OF SAILS.

1. Fore Bunt-Lines.	24. Fore Lower-Topgallant Clew-Lines.	43A. Main Brace-Pendant.
2. " Lower-Topsail Bunt-Lines.	25. " Upper-Topgallant Down-Haul.	44. " Lower-Topsail Brace.
3. " Upper-Topsail Bunt-Lines.	26. " Royal Clew-Line.	44A. " Lower-Topsail Brace-Pendant
4. " Lower-Topgallant Bunt-Lines.	27. Main Lower-Topsail Clew-Line.	45. " Upper-Topsail Brace.
5. " Upper-Topgallant Bunt-Lines.	28. " Upper-Topsail Down-Haul.	45A. " Upper-Topsail Brace-Pendant.
6. " Royal Bunt-Lines.	29. " Lower-Topgallant Clew-Line.	46. " Upper-Topgallant Brace.
7. Main Bunt-Lines.	30. " Upper-Topgallant Down-Haul.	47. " Royal Brace.
8. " Lower-Topsail Bunt-Lines.	31. " Royal Clew-Line.	48. Cro'Jack Brace.
9. " Upper-Topsail Bunt-Lines.	32. Mizen Lower-Topsail Clew-Line.	48A. " Brace-Pendant.
10. " Lower-Topgallant Bunt-Lines.	33. " Upper-Topsail Down-Haul.	49. Mizen Lower-Topsail Brace.
11. " Upper-Topgallant Bunt-Lines.	34. " Lower-Topgallant Clew-Line.	49A. " Lower-Topsail Brace-Pendant.
12. " Royal Bunt-Lines.	35. " Upper-Topgallant Down-Haul.	50. " Upper-Topsail Brace.
13. Cro'Jack Bunt-Lines.	36. " Royal Clew-Line.	50A. " Upper-Topsail Brace-Pendant.
14. Mizen Lower-Topsail Bunt-Lines.	37. Fore Brace.	51. " Lower-Topgallant Brace.
15. " Upper-Topsail Bunt-Lines.	37A. " Brace-Pendant.	52. " Upper-Topgallant Brace.
16. " Lower-Topgallant Bunt-Lines.	38. " Lower-Topsail Brace.	53. " Royal Brace.
17. " Upper-Topgallant Bunt-Lines.	38A. " Lower-Topsail Brace-Pendant.	54. Fore Sheet.
18. " Royal Bunt-Lines.	39. " Upper-Topsail Brace.	55. Main Sheet.
19. Fore Leech-Lines.	39A. " Upper-Topsail Brace-Pendant.	56. Cro'Jack Sheet.
20. Main Leech-Lines.	40. " Lower-Topgallant Brace.	57. Fore Tack.
21. Mizen Leech-Lines.	41. " Upper-Topgallant Brace.	58. Main Tack.
22. Fore Lower-Topsail Clew-Line.	42. " Royal Brace.	59. Cro'Jack Tack.
23. " Upper-Topsail Down-Haul.	43. Main Brace.	

NOTE.—The main lower-topgallant brace has been omitted from the diagram in error, but the lead is the same as on the fore and mizen masts.

97

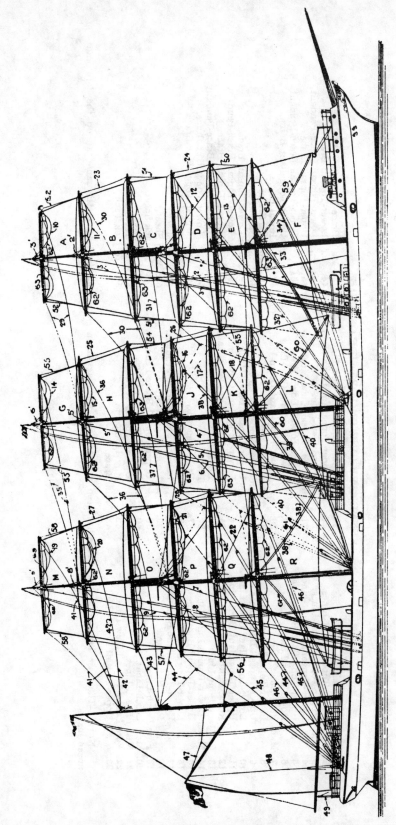

MODERN STEEL FOUR-MAST BARQUE.

Diagram of running rigging on after side of sails.

SQUARE-SAILS AND RUNNING RIGGING OF A FOUR-MAST BARQUE.

A Fore-Royal.
B ,, Upper-Topgallant.
C ,, Lower-Topgallant.
D ,, Upper-Topsail.
E ,, Lower-Topsail.
F ,, Course or Fore-Sail.
G Main-Royal.
H ,, Upper-Topgallant.
I ,, Lower-Topgallant.
J ,, Upper-Topsail.
K ,, Lower-Topsail.
L ,, Course or Main-Sail.
M Mizen-Royal.
N ,, Upper-Topgallant.
O ,, Lower-Topgallant.
P ,, Upper-Topsail.
Q ,, Lower-Topsail.
R ,, Course or Cro'Jack.
1. Fore-Upper-Topsail-Tye and Halliards.
2. ,, Upper-Topgallant-Tye and Halliards.
3. ,, Royal-Tye and Halliards.
4. Main-Upper-Topsail-Tye and Halliards.
5. ,, Upper-Topgallant-Tye and Halliards.
6. ,, Royal-Tye and Halliards.
7. Mizen-Upper-Topsail-Tye and Halliards.
8. ,, Upper-Topgallant-Tye and Halliards.
9. ,, Royal-Tye and Halliards.

10. Fore-Royal-Lifts.
11. ,, Upper-Topgallant-Lifts.
12. ,, Lower-Topgallant-Lifts.
13. Fore-Lifts.
14. Main-Royal-Lifts.
15. ,, Upper-Topgallant-Lifts.
16. ,, Upper-Topsail-Lifts.
17. ,, Lower-Topsail-Lifts.
18. Main-Lifts.
19. Mizen-Royal-Lifts.
20. ,, Upper-Topgallant-Lifts.
21. ,, Upper-Topsail-Lifts.
22. Mizen-Lifts.
23. Fore-Upper-Topgallant-Down-Haul.
24. Fore-Upper-Topsail-Down-Haul.
25. Main-Upper-Topgallant-Down-Haul.
26. Main-Upper-Topsail-Down-Haul.
27. Mizen Upper-Topgallant-Down-Hall.
28. Mizen Upper-Topsail-Down-Hall.
29. Fore-Royal-Braces.
30. ,, Upper-Topgallant-Braces.
31. ,, Upper-Topsail-Braces.
32. ,, Lower-Topgallant-Braces.
33. ,, Lower-Topsail-Braces.
34. Fore-Brace.
35. Main-Royal-Braces.
36. ,, Upper-Topgallant-Braces.

37. Main Lower-Topgallant-Braces.
38. ,, Upper-Topsail-Braces.
39. ,, Lower-Topsail-Braces.
40. Main-Brace.
41. Mizen-Royal-Braces.
42. ,, Upper-Topgallant-Braces.
43. ,, Lower-Topgallant-Braces.
44. ,, Upper-Topsail-Braces.
45. ,, Lower-Topsail-Braces.
46. Mizen-Brace or Cro'Jack-Brace.
47. Spanker-Peak-Halliards and Span.
48. ,, Vangs.
49. ,, Sheets.
50. Fore-Lower-Topsail-Clew-Line.
51. ,, Lower-Topgallant-Clew-Line.
52. ,, Royal-Clew-Line.
53. Main-Lower-Topsail-Clew-Line.
54. ,, Lower-Topgallant-Clew-Line.
55. ,, Royal-Clew-Line.
56. Mizen-Lower-Topsail-Clew-Line.
57. ,, Lower-Topgallant-Clew-Line.
58. ,, Royal-Clew-Line.
59. Fore-Clew-Garnet.
60. Main-Clew-Garnet.
61. Mizen or Cro'Jack-Clew-Garnet.
62. Foot-Ropes.
63. Foot-Ropes Stirrups.

NOTE.—This diagram shows standing lifts on the lower-topsail yards (Nos. 12, 17 and mizen, which is not numbered). This arrangement is not common to all ships, only one or two of the larger ones carrying these lifts.

The tye is that part of the halliard attached to the yard and passing over the sheave in the mast as indicated in the diagram by Nos. 2', 3', etc.

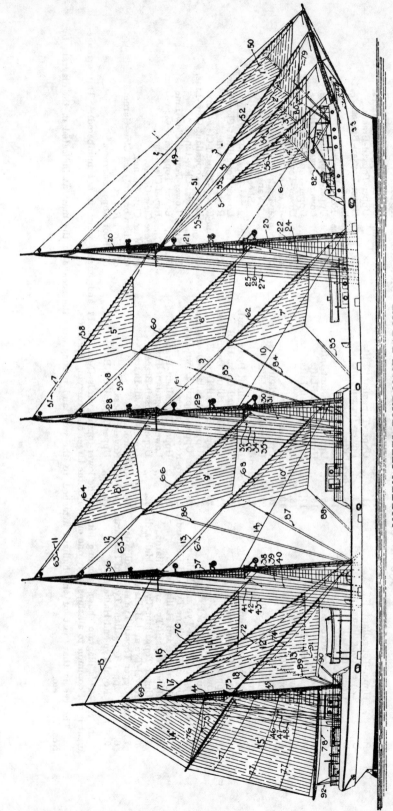

MODERN STEEL FOUR-MAST BARQUE.

Diagram of standing rigging and fore-and-aft sails.

(This drawing shows a vessel with lower-masts and topmasts in one spar.)

STANDING RIGGING AND FORE-AND-AFT SAILS OF A FOUR-MAST BARQUE.

1′ Flying-Jib.
2′ Outer-Jib.
3′ Inner-Jib.
4′ Fore-Topmast-Staysail.
5′ Main-Royal-Staysail.
6′ Main-Topgallant-Staysail.
7′ Main-Topmast-Staysail.
8′ Mizen-Royal-Staysail.
9′ „ Topgallant-Staysail.
10′ „ Topmast-Staysail.
11′ Jigger-Topgallant-Staysail.
12′ „ Topmast-Staysail.
13′ „ Staysail.
14′ „ Topsail.
15′ Spanker.

1. Fore-Royal-Stay.
2. Fore-Topgallant-Stay or Flying-Jib-Stay.
3. Outer-Jib-Stay.
4. Inner-Jib-Stay.
5. Fore-Topmast-Stay.
6. Fore-Stay.
7. Main-Royal-Stay.
8. „ Topgallant-Stay.
9. „ Topmast-Stay.
10. „ Stay.
11. Mizen-Royal-Stay.
12. „ Topgallant-Stay.
13. „ Topmast-Stay.
14. „ Stay.
15. Jigger-Royal-Stay.
16. „ Topgallant-Stay.
17. „ Topmast-Stay.
18. „ Stay.
19. „ Vangs.
20. Fore-Topgallant-Rigging or Shrouds.
21. „ Topmast „ „

22. Fore-Rigging or Shrouds.
23. „ Cap-Stays.
24. „ Topmast-Back-Stays.
25. „ Topmast-Capstay.
26. „ Topgallant-Backstays.
27. „ Royal-Back-Stays.
28. Main-Topgallant Rigging or Shrouds.
29. „ Topmast-Rigging or Shrouds.
30. „ Rigging or Shrouds.
31. „ Capstays.
32. „ Topmast-Backstays.
33. „ Topmast-Cap-Stay.
34. „ Topgallant-Backstays.
35. „ Royal-Backstays.
36. Mizen-Topgallant-Rigging or Shrouds.
37. „ Topmast-Rigging or Shrouds.
38. „ Rigging or Shrouds.
39. „ Cap-Stays.
40. „ Topmast-Backstays.
41. „ Topmast-Cap-Stay.
42. „ Topgallant-Backstays.
43. „ Royal-Backstays.
44. Jigger-Topmast-Rigging or Shrouds.
45. „ Rigging or Shrouds.
46. „ Topmast-Backstays.
47. „ Topgallant-Backstay.
48. „ Royal-Backstay.
49. Flying-Jib-Halliards.
50. Flying-Jib-Down-Haul.
51. Outer-Jib-Halliards.
52. Outer-Jib-Down-Haul.
53. Inner-Jib-Halliards.
54. Inner-Jib-Down-Haul.
55. Fore-Topmast-Staysail-Halliards.
56. Fore-Topmast-Staysail-Down-Haul.
57. Main-Royal-Stays'l-Halliards.

58. Main-Royal-Staysail-Down-Haul.
59. „ Topgallant-Staysail-Halliards.
60. „ Topgallant-Staysail-Down-Haul.
61. „ Topmast-Staysail-Halliards.
62. „ Topmast-Staysail-Down-Haul.
63. Mizen-Royal-Staysail-Halliards.
64. „ Royal-Staysail-Down-Haul.
65. „ Topgallant-Staysail-Halliards.
66. „ Topgallant-Staysail-Down-Haul.
67. „ Topmast-Staysail-Down-Haul.
68. „ Topmast-Staysail-Halliards.
69. Jigger-Topgallant-Staysail-Halliards.
70. „ Topgallant-Staysail-Down-Haul.
71. „ Topmast-Staysail-Halliards.
72. „ Topmast-Staysail-Down-Haul.
73. „ Staysail-Halliards.
74. „ Down-Haul.
75. Spanker-Peak-Halliard and Span.
76. „ Out-Haul.
77. „ Brails.
78. „ Foot-Out-Haul.
79. Flying-Jib-Sheets.
80. Outer-Jib-Sheets.
81. Inner-Jib-Sheets.
82. Fore-Topmast-Staysail-Sheets.
83. Main-Royal-Staysail-Sheets.
84. „ Topgallant-Staysail-Sheet.
85. „ Topmast-Staysail-Sheets.
86. Mizen-Royal-Staysail-Sheets.
87. „ Topgallant-Staysail Sheets.
88. „ Topmast-Staysail-Sheets.
89. Jigger-Topgallant-Staysail-Sheets.
90. „ Staysail-Sheets.
91. „ Topmast-Staysail-Sheets.
92. Spanker-Sheet.

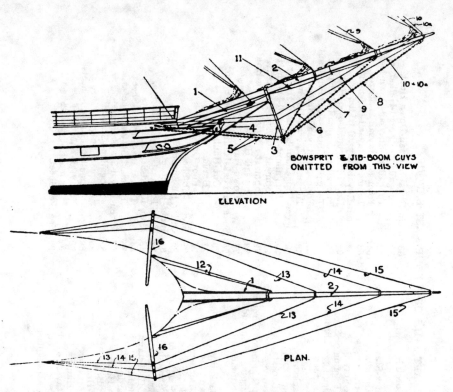

BOWSPRIT & JIB-BOOM GUYS
OMITTED FROM THIS VIEW

ELEVATION

PLAN.

STANDING RIGGING ON BOWSPRIT AND JIB-BOOM.

1. Bowsprit.
2. Jib-boom.
3. Martingale or dolphin-striker.
4. Bobstay.
5. Martingale back-stays or martin-
      gale guys.
6. Inner martingale stay or inner
      jib-boom stay.
7. Outer martingale stay or outer
      jib-boom stay.

8. Flying martingale stay or flying
      jib-boom stay.
9. Outer jibstay.
10. Flying jibstay.
10a. Fore royal stay.
11. Foot-ropes.
12. Bowsprit guys.
13. Inner jib-boom guy.
14. Outer jib-boom guy.
15. Flying jib-boom guy.
16. Whisker booms.

It will be noted that certain headstays, namely Nos. 9, 10 and 10a, pass
through the bowsprit and are led aft to the hull via cleats on either side of
the martingale.

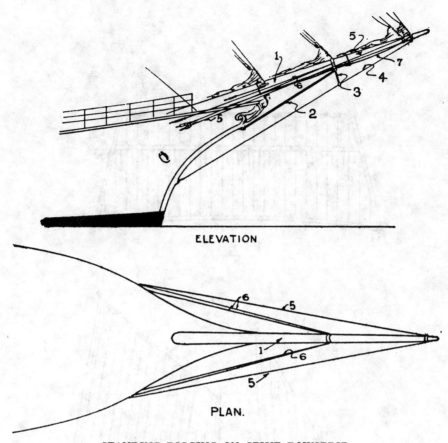

ELEVATION

PLAN.

STANDING RIGGING ON SPIKE BOWSPRIT.

1. Bowsprit.
2. Bobstay.
3. Martingale or dolphin-striker.
4. Outer bobstay.
5. Outer bowsprit guys or jib-boom guys.
6. Bowsprit guys.
7. Foot-ropes.

In this type of bowsprit none of the headstays pass through the spar but all terminate on top, where they are set up tight with metal rigging-screws. In the diagram the latter are hidden below the furled sails.

NOTE.—The martingale is not always fitted on the modern spike bowsprit the barque *Ladas* on page 36 is an example of this.

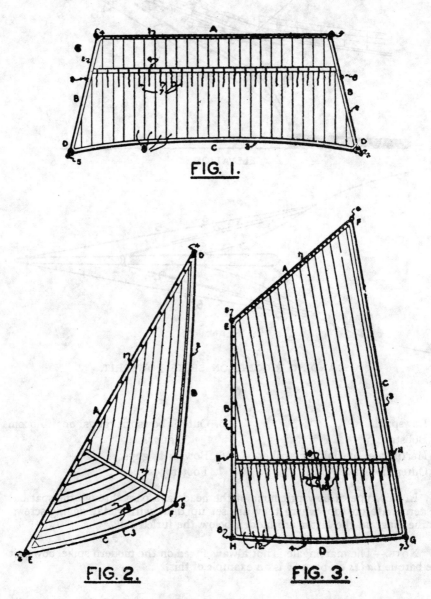

FIG. 1.

FIG. 2.

FIG. 3.

PARTS OF A SAIL.

For key to diagram see opposite page.

PARTS OF A SQUARE SAIL.

FIG. 1.

A Head.
B Leeches.
C Foot.
D Clews.
1. Head-ropes.
2. Leech-ropes.
3. Foot-rope.

4. Head-earing-cringles.
5. Clew-cringles or clew-spectacles.
6. Reef-band.
7. Reef-points.
8. Reef-cringles.
9. Cloths.

NOTE.—Collectively Nos. 1, 2, and 3 are known as boltropes.

PARTS OF A STAYSAIL OR JIB.

FIG. 2.

A Luff, or fore-leech.
B Leech, or after-leech
C Foot.
D Head.
E Tack.
F Clew.
1. Luff-rope, or fore-leech-rope.

2. Leech-rope, or after-leech-rope.
3. Foot-rope.
4. Head-cringle.
5. Clew-cringle.
6. Tack-cringle.
7. Girth-band.
8. Cloths.

NOTE.—Collectively Nos. 1, 2 and 3 are known as boltropes.

PARTS OF A GAFFSAIL.

FIG 3.

A Head.
B Luff, or fore-leech.
C Leech, or after-leech.
D Foot.
E Throat.
F Peak.
G Clew.
H Tack.
1. Head-rope.
2. Luff-rope, or fore-leech-rope.

3. Leech-rope, or after-leech-rope.
4. Foot-rope.
5. Throat-cringle.
6. Peak-cringle.
7. Clew-cringle.
8. Tack-cringle.
9. Reef-band.
10. Reef-points.
11. Reef-cringles.
12. Cloths.

NOTE.—Collectively Nos. 1, 2, 3 and 4 are known as boltropes.

STANDING AND RUNNING RIGGING OF A TWO-MAST TOPSAIL SCHOONER.

Key to Frontispiece.

1. Fore-topgallant-stay (or flying-jib-stay).
2. Flying-jib-halliards.
3. Flying-jib-downhaul.
4. Fore-topmast-stay.
5. Fore-topmast-staysail (or outer-jib) halliards.
6. Fore-topmast-staysail (or outer-jib) downhaul.
7. Inner-jib-stay.
8. Inner-jib-halliards.
9. Inner-jib downhaul.
10. Fore-stay.
11. Fore-staysail-halliards.
12. Fore-staysail downhauls.
13. Flying-jib-sheets.
14. Outer-jib-sheets.
15. Inner-jib-sheets.
16. Fore-staysail-sheets.
17. Upper-topsail-lifts.
18. Upper-topsail-downhauls.
19. Upper-topsail-tye or halliard.
20. Foot-ropes.
21. Foot-ropes stirrup.
22. Upper-topsail-brace.
23. Lower-topsail-clew-line.
24. Lower-topsail-sheets.
25. Fore-yard-lifts.
26. Main-topmast-stay.
27. Main-topmast-staysail-halliard.
28. Main-topmast-staysail-downhaul
29. Main-topmast-staysail-sheet.
30. Fore-peak-halliards.
31. Fore-throat-halliards.
32. Fore-sheet.
33. Fore-boom-topping-lift.
34. Lower-topsail-brace-pendant.
35. Lower-topsail-brace.
36. Fore-brace-pendant.
37. Fore-brace.
38. Main-gaff-topsail-halliard.
39. Main-gaff-topsail-sheet.
40. Main-gaff-topsail-inhaul.
41. Main-gaff-topsail-downhaul.
42. Main peak-halliards
43. Main throat-halliards.
44. Main boom-topping-lift.
45. Main-sheet.
46. Throat-lashing.
47. Peak-lashing.
48. Clew-lashing.
49. Tack-lashing.
50. Bob-stay.
51. Bowsprit-guy.
52. Outer-bobstay.
53. Bowsprit-foot-ropes.
54. Fore-lower-rigging or shrouds.
55. Fore-topmast-rigging or shrouds.
56. Fore-topmast-backstay.
57. Main-lower-rigging or shrouds.
58. Main-topmast-shroud.
59. Mast-hoops.
60. Reef-cringles.
61. Reef-points.
62. Sheer-poles.
63. Chain-plates.
64. Signal-halliards.
65. Dead-eyes and lanyards.
66. Main-spreader.
67. Triatic-stay.

For names of sails see page 94.

SECTION IV.

A Glossary of Technical Terms used in connection
with Masts, Sails, Spars and Rigging.

GLOSSARY

Abaft.—Behind, or nearer to the stern.

Angulated Sails.—A term used to describe a jib or staysail having cloths running parallel to both leech and foot, forming an angle at the girth-band, as on page 104.

Backstays.—Stays leading from the upper part of a topmast, topgallant-mast royal-mast, or skysail-mast down to the ship's side abaft the lower rigging.

Balanced Lug.—A lug-sail fitted with boom and yard, both of which are attached to the mast and project short distance to the fore side of it. This sail remains on one side of the mast and is not dipped when going about.

Belaying-Pins.—Wood or metal pins inserted in holes in the pin-rail. Used for belaying running-rigging.

Block.—A shell of wood or metal, in which are one or more sheaves, over which a rope is rove to form a purchase.

Bobstays.—Stays extending between the outer end of the bowsprit and the vessel's stem, to counteract the upward pull of the head-stays. (Pages 102 and 103.)

Boltrope.—A rope sewn round the edges of a sail to strengthen it; that at the head of the sail being the head-rope, that on the leeches the leech rope, on the foot the foot-rope.

Bonnet.—A small additional sail attached to the foot of a staysail, gaffsail or jib in calm weather to increase its area.

Boom.—A small spar, or the spar used to extend the foot of a gaffsail, trysail or jib; studding sail booms are spars provided to extend the yards to carry studding sails.

Boom Topping Lift.—A rope led from the end of the boom of a gaffsail over a block at the masthead and down to a purchase at the deck, to support the boom when reefing, or when the sail is furled. (Page 106.)

Bowline.—A rope used to keep taut the weather leech of a square sail when close-hauled. It is led forward to the mast in front, or in the case of the foresail, to the bowsprit.

Braces.—Ropes leading from the yardarm to the vessel's side or adjacent mast, by means of which the yards are hauled to any required position.

Brace Pendants.—Short pieces of rope, one end of which is attached to the yardarm, the other having a block through which the brace leads.

Brails.—Ropes on each side of a sprit-sail, spanker or trysail, leading through blocks at the mast and by means of which the sail is gathered to the mast.

Bumkin.—A short spar of wood or iron projecting from the ship's side, to which the lower brace blocks are attached. Also in yachts, a small spar projecting over the stern and corresponding to the bowsprit, to which the mizen sheet block is attached.

Bunt.—The middle cloths of a square sail; also the part of a furled sail which is on the centre of the yard.

Bunt-Gasket.—A net or canvas apron used to fasten the bunt of a square-sail to the yard when furled.

Bunt Lines.—Ropes leading from the foot of a square-sail through a block at the head and down to the deck. Used to haul up the middle lower part of the sail when furling.

Cap.—A fitting or band used to connect the head of one mast to the lower portion of the mast above, also at the outer end of the bowsprit to support the jib-boom.

Cap-stay.—A backstay leading from the mast cap to the ship's side.

Chafing-Gear.—See *Puddening*.

Chain-Plates.—Iron bars bolted to the ship's side and to which the dead-eyes, or rigging screws, of the lower rigging and backstays are attached.

Channels.—Wooden structures projecting from the sides of the older type of wooden vessel and used to give greater spread to the lower rigging and backstays; in more modern vessels chain plates take the place of channels.

Cheeks.—Flat plates of iron or wood, bolted to the sides of the mast to form angle supports below the top or cross-trees and to take the weight of the mast above.

Clew.—The lower corners of a square-sail, and the after lower corner of a fore-and-aft sail.

Clew-Garnets.—Ropes used to gather the clews of the courses up to the centre of the yard when furling the sail.

Clew-Lines.—Lines or ropes by means of which the clews of the upper square-sails are hauled up to their respective yards. In some ships the sail is clewed up to the bunt or centre of the yard, and others to the yardarms.

Cock-Billed.—A yard is said to be cock-billed when it is canted up at an angle to the horizontal.

Crance-Iron.—An iron band at the outer end of a bowsprit or jibboom to which the stays, etc., are attached.

Cringle.—A ring or loop in the boltrope of a sail.

Cross-Trees.—Wood or iron spars fitted across the cheeks and trestle-trees to support the top, also the term applied to the lower portion of the top-gallant doubling.

Dead-Eyes.—Circular wooden blocks, with three holes through which the lanyards, used in setting up taut the shrouds and backstays, are rove. Round the outer circumference is a groove which takes the end of the shroud or chain-plate strop and shackle.

Dolphin-Striker.—See *Martingale*.

Doublings.—A term applied to the overlapping portions of a built-up mast, as between the top and the lower-cap; and the cross-trees and the topmast cap.

Downhaul.—A rope leading from the head of a sail down to the deck, by means of which the sail is hauled down for furling.

Driver.—The gaffsail on the after mast of a ship or barque.

Earing.—A term given to the outer corners of the head of a square-sail, also the rope or line by means of which the corner is lashed to the yard.

Earing-Cringle.—A cringle at the upper corners of a square-sail, through which the earing or lashing is passed.

Eyes of Rigging.—The loops or bights at the end of stays or shrouds which are passed over the masthead.

Fake.—One turn in a coil of rope.

Fall.—The running end of a tackle or purchase; the moving parts of a tackle or purchase.

Fid.—A short piece of wood or iron resting over the cross-trees and through a hole in the mast to keep it in position.

Fife-Rail.—A rail on stanchions at the foot of a mast and fitted with belaying-pins.

Flemish-Horse.—A short foot-rope at the extreme end of a yard. (See lower-yards on sail plan of ship *Coriolanus*.)

Foot of Sail.—The lower edge of a sail.

Foot-Rope.—On a sail; the boltrope sewn to the lower edge or foot of the sail. On a yard or bowsprit; a rope suspended below it on which the sailors stand when furling, reefing, or working on the sails.

Fore-and-aft Sails.—All staysails, gaffsails, lugsails, etc. all of which are set in a fore and aft direction, *i.e.* along the centre line of the vessel.

Fore-and-aft Rig.—Any vessel rigged with fore and aft sails.

Fore-Mast.—The mast nearest the bow in all vessels of two or more masts where there is a larger mast abaft it. Where the mast nearest the bow is the largest, as in the case of a ketch, it becomes a main and no fore-mast is carried.

Furl.—To roll a sail on to its yard or boom and bind it there with gaskets.

Futtock Shrouds.—Iron rods or stays leading from the mast to the rim of the top or crosstrees to take the pull of the upper rigging.

Gaff.—The spar along the head of a fore and-aft-sail. It is hoisted to the correct angle by means of the peak and throat halliards. *Standing Gaff*—A gaff which remains aloft, the sail being brailed in when not required, instead of lowering the gaff.

Gaff-Jaws.—Jaws on the inner end of a hoisting gaff, which partly encircle the mast and prevent the gaff from falling away to leeward.

Gaff-Topsail.—A fore-and-aft topsail set abaft the topmast, its foot being spread by the gaff.

Gammon Iron.—An iron band holding the bowsprit down to the stem of the vessel. In small craft an iron ring at the stem, through which the running bowsprit passes.

Gaskets.—Short pieces of line used to bind a sail to the yard when furled.

Gooseneck.—An iron universal joint used to attach a boom or spar to the mast in such a manner that it is free to move in any direction.

Gores.—Angular pieces in a sail to increase its width at certain parts.

Grommet.—A ring of rope.

Guy.—A rope or stay leading to the side of the vessel, a rope used to steady a boom.

109

Halliard, or **Halyard.**—Rope, or gear, by means of which a sail, yard, gaff, flag etc., is hoisted.

Hanks.—Rings on a stay, to which a staysail is attached and which enable it to be hoisted up along the stay.

Head-Sails.—The jibs and staysails set between the bowsprit and the fore; in some cases the main-mast. Sometimes used to include the square-sails on the fore-mast of a square-rigged vessel.

Head-Stays.—Stays between the bowsprit and the foremost mast.

Heel of the Mast.—The lower part of the mast which rests in the mast step.

Heel of the Bowsprit.—The inner end of the bowsprit.

Heel-Rope.—A rope passed round the heel of the jib-boom and used for hauling it out. Also a rope used to lash the inner end of a studding sail boom.

Hoisting Yards.—Yards which are hoisted and lowered in setting and furling the sails, as in the case of upper topsails, upper-topgallant, and royal yards.

Hoops, Mast-Hoops.—Wooden rings which encircle the mast, and to which the luff of a gaffsail is attached.

Horn Bowsprit.—A single spar bowsprit and jib-boom; a single spar standing bowsprit; a spike bowsprit.

Horse.—A rope, timber or iron bar, running across the deck, on which the sheet block of a fore-and-aft sail slides, allowing the sail to traverse from side to side without casting off the sheet.

Hounds.—A change in diameter of the mast to form a rest for the eyes of the rigging, crosstrees, etc.

Jackstay.—An iron bar or wire along the top of a yard, or the after side of a mast and to which the sail is made fast.

Jib.—A staysail set on a head-stay.

Jib-boom.—A spar fitted along the top of the bowsprit and projecting beyond it, to which the outer head-stays are set up.

Jib-Headed-Sail.—A triangular sail with a head like a jib or staysail.

Jigger-Mast.—The after mast on a four-masted vessel.

Jimmy Green.—A square-sail set below the bowsprit, used during the clipper period.

Lacing.—A line used to attach a staysail to the stay in such a manner that it will be free to slide.

Lanyard.—A short piece of light rope or line rove through dead-eyes for the purpose of setting taut a shroud or backstay.

Lashing.—A piece of rope by means of which two objects are made fast; as lashing two spars together.

Lateen Sail.—A triangular sail shaped like a jib or staysail but having a yard along the luff, or fore leech. The sail is set in the same manner as the dipping lug, the tack and fore end of the yard being made fast to the stem or deck. This rig is common to the Mediterranean and the East.

Leech.—The vertical edges of a sail. In fore-and-aft sails the fore leech, or leading edge, is usually known as the luff.

Leech-Lines.—Ropes leading from the leeches of a square-sail, through block above the yard and down to the deck, and used to control and gather in the sail for furling.

Lifts.—Ropes used to support or trim a yard or boom, those for the yards leading from the yardarms to blocks on the mast, and so to the deck; for those on a boom see "Boom-topping-lift." *Standing Lifts* are ropes leading from the yardarms to the mast but in this case they are shackled there instead of leading down to the deck. These lifts are used to take the weight of the yardarms of hoisting yards when the sails are furled. See perspective drawings on pages 84 and 85.

Lower-Mast.—The lowest section of a built-up mast. The section on which the course is carried.

Lubber-Hole.—An opening in the decking of the *top* on either side of the mast and giving access to the *top* without passing over the rim and futtock shrouds.

Luff or Fore Leech.—The leading edge of a fore-and-aft sail.

Main-Mast.—The principal mast in a vessel. In large craft usually the second mast from the bow; in ketches and yawls, the first mast from the bow.

Man-Rope.—A life-line; a line rigged above the bowsprit and jib-boom to provide a hand grip for men working on the spar; the ropes round the side of a life-boat, for persons in the water to hold on to.

Martingale.—A wood or iron spar projecting down from below the bowsprit cap to give greater spread to the stays below the spar; in modern ships with spike bowsprit, a short iron bar between the underside of the spar and the outer bobstay. Gives additional strength to bowsprit and jib-boom and counteracts the upward pull of the head-stays.

Mast-Bands.—Iron bands round a mast; the lower ones often fitted with belaying-pins. See *Spider Bands.*

Mast-Hoops.—See *Hoops.*

Mizen-Mast.—In large vessels the third mast from the bow; in ketches, yawls, etc., the small after-mast.

Mousing.—A lashing of small line across the open part of a hook to prevent it from coming adrift.

Painter.—A rope attached to the stem of a boat, used for making fast, or towing astern of another craft.

Parcelling.—Long narrow strips of tarred canvas wound spirally round a rope prior to serving.

Parrel.—A hoop, band, or other gear used to hold a hoisting yard to the mast and allowing the yard to be raised or lowered as required.

Peak.—The upper after corner of a gaffsail. This term is also used to describe the outer end of the gaff; thus a flag hoisted to a block on the end of the gaff is said to be at the peak.

Peak Signal Halliards.—A light line leading through a block at the outer end of the gaff and used for hoisting a flag.

Pendant (pronounced pennant).—A short length of wire or rope with a block at one end, the other being attached to yard, boom or other fixing; example: *Brace Pendant*.

Pin-Rail.—A rail fixed inside the bulwarks with holes for belaying-pins.

Pole.—That portion of a mast between the highest rigging and the truck.

Pole-Mast.—A mast formed of one single spar from keel to truck; example the mizen-mast of the barque *Ladas* on page 36.

Preventer-Stay.—A temporary or additional stay. A stay not forming part of the standing rigging.

Puddening.—Chafing gear: old rope, canvas, oakum, rope-yarns, etc., made up to required shape and fixed on stays, rails, etc., to prevent chafing the sails.

Purchase.—A combination of blocks and falls arranged to increase the lifting or hauling power on a rope.

Quarter (of a yard).—That portion of the yard between the centre and yardarm.

Quarter-Iron.—An iron band round the yard at the quarter.

Rake.—The angle or inclination—in a fore-and-aft direction—between the centre line of a mast and the perpendicular.

Ratlines.—Small ropes running horizontally across the shrouds to form ladders for getting aloft.

Reach.—To sail with the wind abeam or moderately close-hauled.

Reef.—To reduce the area of a sail by tying part of it up to its yard or boom.

Reef-Band.—A strip of canvas across the sail to provide additional strength at the reef-points.

Reef-Points.—Short lengths of light line rove through eyelet-holes in the reef-band. They are of equal length on either side of the sail and are used for tying the reefed portion to the yard.

Reef-Tackle.—A tackle between the reef cringles on the sail and the yard or boom and used to haul out and stretch the reef band while tying the points.

Reef-Tackle-Patch.—An additional piece of canvas sewn on a sail near the reef tackle cringle for extra strength.

Reeve.—To pass a rope through a block or sheave hole.

Rigging-Screw.—A tension screw having a right and left hand thread, one end is attached to the chain-plate and the other to the lower end of the stay or shroud. Used in place of dead-eyes and lanyards for setting up the rigging. Also a clamp used to hold two parts of a rope together while a seizing is being put on.

Ring-Tail.—A sail set abaft a boom or gaffsail in fine weather to increase its area.

Rim of the Top.—The binding band round the outer edge of the top.

Royal.—The sail on the royal mast; the sail above the topgallant sail.

Royal-Mast.—The mast above the topgallant; in modern ships the topgallant-mast and royal-mast are formed of one single spar, but are divided by the topgallant-hounds.

Running-Bowsprit.—A bowsprit which can be hauled inboard when not in use; example: sail plan of Brixham trawler *Valerian.*

Running-Rigging.—Any rigging which is used to operate the sails or gear of a vessel; braces, bunt-lines, clew-lines, halliards, etc.; any rigging which runs through blocks or is moved in any way, as distinct from *Standing Rigging.*

Seize.—To bind two ropes or other objects together with small line.

Sennit.—A cord formed of ropeyarns or spunyarn and plaited by hand; there are various forms of sennit according to the method of plaiting used.

Serve.—To wind spun-yarn round a rope to prevent chafing.

Shackle.—A link with one end closed by a bolt. Used to join two chains or eyes together.

Sheave.—The roller or pulley inside a block. A grooved pulley over which a rope passes.

Sheave-Hole.—A hole or slot in a spar, fitted with a sheave, as in the case of the sheave-holes in the masts through which the halliards or tye pass.

Sheer-Pole, Sheer-Batten.—A wood or iron bar fixed in a horizontal direction across the shrouds just above the dead-eyes or rigging-screws.

Sheet.—A rope or chain from the lower corners or clews of a square-sail, led down to the deck; a rope or tackle from the after end of the boom of a gaffsail to the deck; a rope or tackle from the clew of a staysail or jib to the deck. The object of the sheet is to control the free portion of the sail.

Shrouds.—The standing rigging between the lower-masthead and the ship's side; the standing rigging between the topmast-head and the rim of the top; the standing rigging between the topgallant-masthead and the cross-trees.

Signal-Halliards.—A light line leading through a block or sheave hole at the truck or gaff end and used for hoisting flags.

Skysail.—The sail above the royal.

Skysail-Mast.—The mast above the royal-mast.

Sling.—A chain supporting the centre of a lower yard. *Slings.*—A term used to describe the centre of the yard.

Span.—A rope fixed at both ends with a block or thimble running on it to which a block or tackle is attached; example: the span on a gaff for the outer blocks of the peak halliards.

Spanker.—See *Driver.*

Spencer.—A fore-and-aft sail carried on the fore and main-masts of a full-rigged ship.

Spider Band.—An iron band round the mast just above the deck and fitted with belaying-pins.

Spider Hoop.—See *Spider Band.*

Spinnaker.—A large triangular sail used in yachts when running, and set from the masthead to a boom over the beam.

I

Spreaders.—Wood or iron bars forming struts for the rigging. They are used to counteract the pull of the sails on a spar. Spreaders are used on the backstays of large vessels and are fitted at the cross-trees; in fore-and-aft rigged vessels and small craft they are at the head of the lower-mast.

Spike-Bowsprit.—See *Horn-Bowsprit.*

Sprit.—A spar running diagonally across a sprit-sail to support the peak; example the sail plan of the barge *Lady Daphne* on page 72.

Sprit-Sail.—A fore-and-aft sail shaped like a gaffsail but not fitted with a gaff. The sail is extended by a spar or sprit running diagonally across it. At one time the term applied to a square-sail carried below the bowsprit.

Square-Sails.—A term given to all sails carried on yards running across the vessel, as distinct from fore-and-aft sails which are on the fore and aft centre line.

Square-Rig.—A vessel is said to be square-rigged when she has one or more masts with a complete range of square-sails. A topsail schooner is not classified as square-rigged as she has only upper square-sails.

Standing-Bowsprit.—A bowsprit which is built into the vessel and remains permanently in position, as distinct from the running bowsprit which can be hauled inboard when required.

Standing-Part.—The fixed end of a rope or gear.

Standing Rigging.—That part of the rigging which acts as a support to the masts and spars. Rigging which is not moved when operating the vessel.

Stays.—Wire or rope used to support the masts in a fore-and-aft or thwartship direction.

Staysail.—A triangular sail set on a fore and aft stay; jibs are staysails.

Steeving.—The angle or slope which the bowsprit makes to the horizontal.

Stirrups.—Short ropes hanging from the yard or spar at regular intervals to support the foot-rope.

Strop, or *Strap.*—A piece of rope or an iron band passed round a block or dead-eye; also a ring of rope or chain.

Studding Sail.—A light sail set outside a square-sail, the head being attached to a small spar or studding sail yard. This yard is carried by the studding sail boom which is expended from the yardarm. Studding sails are used to increase the sail area when running.

Tabernacle, or *Mast Trunk.*—A casing built into the vessel and enclosing the lower portion of the mast and in which the mast is pivoted. The tabernacle allows the mast to be lowered to the deck for passing under bridges, etc. This type of mast step is used by inland craft.

Tack.—The forward lower corner of a fore and-aft-sail; a rope or purchase by means of which the clew of a course is kept down.

Tacking.—Beating to windward.

Tackle.—A combination of blocks and ropes to form a purchase.

Thimble.—A round or heart-shaped ring of iron, grooved on the outer edge and inserted into an eye-splice at the end of a rope to prevent chafing.

Throat.—The inner top corner of a gaffsail.

Toggle.—A wooden pin tapered at each end, with a groove round the centre which is spliced into the end of a rope, by passing the toggle through a becket or loop in the other end of the rope the ends are joined; example: flags are attached to signal halliards by means of toggles.

Top.—A semi-circular platform of wood or iron built on the trestle-trees at the head of the lower-mast; it gives spread to the topmast rigging and forms a handy working space aloft.

Topgallant-Mast.—The mast above the topmast. See *Royal-Mast.*

Topmast.—The mast above the lower-mast.

Topping Lift.—See *Boom-Topping-Lift.*

Traveller.—A ring sliding on a horse or stay to facilitate the movement of the sail or sheet.

Trestle-Trees.—Wood or iron (angle iron) fitted in a fore-and-aft direction on top of the cheeks or at the hounds and supporting the cross-trees and top.

Triatic-Stay.—A stay largely used in fore-and-aft rigged vessels; it extends horizontally from the cap of one mast to the cap of the next.

Tricing-Line.—A light line attached to the tack of a gaffsail and led up to a block at the gaff-jaws thence to the deck. It is used to haul, or trice, up the tack to any height above the boom.

Truck.—The circular piece of wood at the top of the highest mast and provided with a sheave for the signal halliards.

Trysail.—A spencer of a ship or barque (see *Spencer.*) The spanker of a brig or snow; a smaller sail set as a storm sail in place of a gaffsail in a fore-and-aft rigged vessel.

Tye.—That part of a halliard which passes over the sheave in the masthead. usually made of chain, one end shackled to the slings of the yard, the other—after being rove through the block or sheave hole—being shackled to the halliard.

Unbend.—To cast off and remove the sails from the spars. To cast off a rope.

Vangs.—Ropes leading from the outer end of a gaff or sprit to the deck at either side of the vessel, usually fitted with a purchase at the lower end Used to steady and control the spar.

Water Sails.—Later known as a *Jimmy Greens.* A square-sail carried below the bowsprit.

Worming.—To wind ropeyarn or spunyarn round a rope for the purpose of filling up the strands. The yarn is laid spirally round the rope in the grooves formed by the strands.

Yard.—The spar on which a square-sail is set. See *Square-Sail.*

Yardarm.—The outer ends of a yard.

APPENDIX

SAILING SHIP DRAWINGS.

THE publishers can supply sets of sailing ship plans specially drawn by the Author to scales suitable for model construction, and consisting of Lines Drawing; General Arrangement Drawing with Deck Plans; Sail and Rigging Plan including all running-rigging, and, in certain cases, additional sheets providing scale details of individual deck fittings, masts, spars, rigging, etc.

The aim of these drawings is to provide authentic data for those interested in the sailing ship period, or desiring to build models of named ships. They are based on original drawings and specifications, from which all essential information has been condensed into three or more sheets of convenient size averaging 30 ins. × 22 ins.

With a view to illustrating the ship as she actually went to sea, the original details have been edited as far as possible by personal survey of such vessels as were available, from the author's own records and research work, or both, but the author will always be pleased to learn of any changes which, through lack of information, may not have been embodied or noted on the drawings, so that such information can be added.

The undermentioned ships are at present available, together with a few sets for the construction of simple models not intended to represent any particular vessel.

Acamas.—Steel full-rigged ship. A large modern ship rigged vessel of 1860 tons.

Admiral Karpfanger.—Steel four-mast barque, better known under her original name of *L'Avenir.*

Albert Rickmers.—Steel three-mast barque. This is a good example of the modern three-mast barque, she is perhaps better remembered as *Penang.*

Almirante Saldanha.—This aux steel four-masted barquentine, employed as a Brazilian training ship, is of most modern design and a very good subject for a beautiful model.

Archibald Russell.—Steel four-mast barque. A very well known unit of the grain fleet and a frequent visitor to this country in the last days of sail.

Carl Vinnen.—Steel auxiliary five-mast two-topsail schooner. This vessel has already been mentioned and illustrated in this book.

Comte de Smet de Naeyer.—Full-rigged ship built as a Belgian training ship.

Coriolanus.—Iron full-rigged ship. The *Coriolanus* was known as "Queen of the Jute Clippers" and is said to have been one of the most beautiful iron ships ever turned out.

Cromdale.—Steel full-rigged ship. A very fine example of one of the later day wool clippers.

Cutty Sark.—This famous tea clipper needs no further description.

Dammark.—A beautiful full-rigger and well known training ship.

Eagle.—Barque-rigged American training ship, once the German training ship *Gorch Fock* (*I*).

Emma Ernest.—Wood three-mast topsail schooner. A typical coaster and a vessel well known to Londoners as the *Seven Seas*, moored off the Embankment.

Endeavour.—Bark (1768) this is Captain Cook's famous vessel and these drawings are very fully detailed as the result of careful research work, and really authentic and suitable for perfect scale models.

Falken.—A modern yacht-like fore-and-aft schooner, built as a training ship for the Swedish Navy. Would make a good sailing scale model.

Fame.—Composite brig. This is one of the Bengal Pilot Brigs. (see Hoogly Pilot Brig).

Formby.—Steel-full-rigged ship. Reputed to have been the first vessel to be constructed of steel.

France (*II.*).—Steel auxiliary five-mast barque. This, the second five-mast barque of that name, was the largest sailing craft ever built.

Georg Stage (*I*). This little steam auxiliary full-rigged ship was a training ship in Denmark and later became the British *Joseph Conrad*.

Gladan.—Sister ship of the schooner *Falken*.

Gorch Fock (*I*).—Steel auxiliary barque, later the American training ship *Eagle*.

Grossherzog Friedrich August.—This was one of the most beautiful training ships ever built, was originally German but is now the Norwegian *Statsraad Lehmkual*.

Halcyon.—Steel lee-board ketch. The *Halcyon* is a modern coasting ketch of the barge type.

Harriet MacGregor.—Famous Tasmanian clipper barque, well known for her passages between Tasmania and London.

Helen Barnet Gring.—A typical American four-mast fore and aft schooner.

Herzogin Cecilie.—This fine four-masted barque was perhaps the most famous and most photographed vessel of the last days of sail.

Joseph Conrad.—This beautiful little "frigate-built" ship was owned by Alan Villiers and is the subject of his book "The cruise of the *Conrad*."

Juan Sebastian De Elcano.—Steel four-mast topsail-schooner. This Spanish Training Ship was designed in Great Britain and is an extremely fine looking craft and an excellent subject for a model.

Kaiwo Maru.—Steel auxiliary fourmasted barque in the training service of Japan.

Kommodore Johnsen.—Steel auxiliary four-masted barque, ex *Magdalene Vinnen* and one of the best known training ships in the last days of sail.

Lady Daphne.—200-ton Thames sailing barge. This is a typical example of the large coasting barge so well known on the South coast.

Lady of Avenel.—A fine little wood brigantine, built as a British coaster and later converted into a yacht.

L'Avenir.—Steel four-masted barque, originally a famous Belgian training ship, but also well known as one of the regular grain ships in the last days of sail.

Leon.—Wood brigantine. This is a particularly pleasing brigantine of the larger class, with raised quarterdeck and trunk-cabin. This set also includes a full construction plan for a plank on frame model.

Loch Etive.—Iron full-rigged ship. One of the famous "Loch Line" clippers.

Loch Sunnart.—Iron full-rigged ship. Sister ship of *Loch Etive.*

Magdalene Vinnen (II.).—Steel auxiliary four-mast barque. This is the second four-mast barque of that name and is a typical modern ship with mid-ship bridge deck.

Marie Sophie.—Wood brig. The *Marie Sophie* is a good example of the trading brig in her prime.

Muirneag.—Zulu type fishing vessel. These drawings consist of a full set of constructional plans for the actual vessel. The original drawings were produced by the author for presentation to the Society for Nautical Research as a detailed record of this almost extinct type, and were compiled from a full survey of the ship.

Mount Stewart.—Steel full-rigged ship. Sister ship of *Cromdale.*

Mozart.—Steel four-mast barquentine. A well-known and typical example of the modern steel barquentine.

Nippon Maru.—Steel auxiliary four-masted barque, sister ship of *Kaiwo Maru.*

Oamaru.—Iron full-rigged ship. This was one of the famous colonial clippers, and a good looking ship, with long poop and fine lines.

Parma.—Steel four-masted barque, well remembered as regular grain trader to this country, and the subject of Alan Villiers' well known book of ship photographs, *"Last of the Wind Ships".*

Penang.—Steel three-mast barque. (Ex-*Albert Rickmers*).

Pommern.—Steel four-mast barque. Another old friend and regular visitor with the grain ships.

Queen Margaret.—Steel four-mast barque, referred to by Lubbock as "one of the fastest and most beautiful carriers of the nineties".

Raven.—Wood brigantine. A good example of the trading brigantine once so common in both off shore and coasting trades.

Ross-Shire.—Steel four-mast barque. A well remembered member of Thomas Law's fleet of sailing ships.

Runnymede.—Wood snow. This is an interesting old stager with square stern and single topsails.

Statsraad Lehmkual.—Steel three-mast barque. A typical modern training ship.

Three Brothers.—Rye smack. Ketch rigged.

Timaru.—Iron full-rigged ship. Sister ship to the iron clipper *Oamaru*.

Torrens.—Composite ship. Well known as the favourite ship of Joseph Conrad.

True Briton.—This famous Blackwaller would make a fine subject for model making.

Valerian.—Brixham trawler. This is a very comprehensive set with a view to providing all possible details of these fine boats.

Waterwitch.—Wood three-mast barquentine. Another old favourite of the British coast, she was the last real square-rigger on the coast.

William Ashburner.—Three-masted topsail-schooner, one of the last sailing ships in our coastal trade and still well remembered.

COASTING KETCH.—A full set of plans for a trader such as that shown in the Plate facing page 67 of this book.

COASTING SCHOONER.—This is a typical two-mast Topsail-schooner. The sail plan of which is shown in plate 44.

SCANDINAVIAN BARQUENTINE.—This is one of the beautiful little Baltic barquentines which used to be regular visitors to this country.

74-GUN SHIP.—These plans, to a scale of $\frac{3}{16}''$ to 1 ft., are perhaps the most complete set of drawings ever published of one of these old two-deckers. The set includes Profile, Longitudinal and many Cross Sections; End Views, and plans of each deck. There are also separate drawings of each component forming the various masts and spars, together with the position of blocks, rigging sequence and the lead of the gear. Alternative Rigging Plans are available, one with sails bent and the other for models with bare yards and the lighter gear rigged-down. Details of guns, boats, anchors, etc., are also available. These are plans of the actual ship, not simplified model drawings.

HOOGLY PILOT BRIG.—These brigs will be remembered by all who served in the Calcutta trade in the days of sail, and the plans, which are to a scale of $\frac{1}{8}''=1'\ 0'$, are from the original builders' drawings.

SCOTTISH ZULU—The Zulu was perhaps the finest of all Scottish fishing types, and these plans, to a scale of $\frac{1}{2}''=1'\ 0'$, were compiled by the author for preservation by the Society for Nautical Research They are full constructional drawings of the *Muirneag*, taken off the actual vessel while she was being broken up, and when many constructional details otherwise hidden were exposed. Full fitting out specifications are included, as well as many notes and sketches.

12 GUN BRIG OF WAR.—This set has been produced for super detail $\frac{1}{4}$ in. scale models of one of the old 12 gun brigs, which many will remember as sail training ships in the Royal Navy.

40-GUN FRIGATE.—The frigate was the cruiser of the Sailing Navy, and these plans are extremely fully detailed and suitable for the construction of a perfect scale model.

THREE-MASTED TOPSAIL SCHOONER.—Drawings of a typical schooner in her clipper days.

ELIZABETHAN GALLEON.—Suitable for a small decorative model, typical of the Elizabethan period.

RING NET BOAT.—One of the modern cruiser sterned fishermen of the Scottish coast.

SHIPS BOATS.—A range of details including Lines, Sections, Construction Plans and details of ships boats as carried by the sailing Man-of-War.

MUZZLE LOADING GUNS.—A range of old time muzzle loading guns as carried in the days of sail.

MASTING & RIGGING.—Large scale prints of the working drawings which form many of the plates in the book *Masting & Rigging* are available. These cover mast and spar construction, fittings and ironwork, rigging details, and fairlead diagrams. The scales range from $1\frac{1}{2}''$ to $3''$ to the foot, and the average size of the sheet is about $30'' \times 22''$.

WINCHES, WINDLASS, AND STEERING GEAR.—Large scale prints are available of some of the plates of the above fittings as published in the book *Deep-Water Sail*.

Particulars on application to : Brown, Son & Ferguson, Ltd., 52 Darnley Street, Glasgow, G41 2SG

INDEX

123

PAGE FOR READER'S OWN RECORDS

Ship's Name	Rig	Notes and Remarks

PAGE FOR READER'S OWN RECORDS

Ship's Name	Rig	Notes and Remarks

126